THE WHOLE TRUTH

CARRIE MONROE O'KEEFE

Cover art by Dan Burdeski.

Paperback: 978-1-7336299-0-4
Ebook: 978-1-7336299-1-1
Library of Congress Control Number: 2019931583

For Signa & Sophia

1

GINNY

Ginny Ross rode her bike over the fallen red leaves of the Sugar Maple trees that lined her driveway. Then she turned left onto Virginia Avenue. The streets were quiet. She took advantage of the early hour and zigzagged down the middle of the streets, the bright leaves swirling behind her, until she got close to Main Street. She rode through two intersections, both with red flashing lights, and slowed to a stop in front of The Drip. She leaned her bike against the brick building, not bothering to lock it at this hour, and pushed open the glass door, causing a bell to jingle.

"Be right out," a familiar woman's voice hollered from the back. Ginny walked to the counter and looked at the day's pastry options. Scones, bagels, muffins, and sticky cinnamon rolls filled the display case. She settled on a jumbo-sized blueberry muffin and set it down near the register.

Rachel Kelly, a round woman with chestnut-brown hair, came up front and smiled, producing deep dimples in her cheeks.

"Hot chocolate? Your red nose must mean it's still cold out!" Before Ginny could answer, Rachel grabbed a large green paper cup and started making hot chocolate.

"Yes, please," Ginny said, pulling dollar bills and quarters from her backpack.

"You're early this week," Rachel yelled over the sound of the milk being frothed.

"I have a project to work on," Ginny said, pretending to count her money. She wasn't sure if she was a good liar; she didn't do it often. Rachel finished up the drink with a generous pile of whipped cream and chocolate shavings and put the muffin in a thin paper bag.

"Is your mom flying anywhere exotic this weekend?" She took Ginny's money and stamped the last blank coffee cup on the frequent visitor card Ginny put on the counter, winking as she handed it back.

Ginny thought for a second as she slid the card back into her wallet. When her mom was preparing to leave Friday morning, Ginny was so distracted she didn't pay much attention. "Paris, I think?"

"Oooh la la! Hopefully she'll bring you back something good!"

"Hopefully! Thanks, Ms. Kelly." Ginny grabbed a couple of napkins and shoved them and her muffin into her backpack as she triggered the bell again. She put her cup in the bottle cage of her bike and climbed back on. She rode a few doors down and hopped off next to a bike rack that lined the sidewalk in front of Book Nook. After locking her bike, she grabbed her hot chocolate and walked to the door. When it didn't open, she stepped back to check the store's hours on the large front window. *Sunday: 10am-10pm.* She looked at her watch and then heard the door being unlocked.

"What's the rush?" It was Pete Howard, a college student who came home on weekends to work at the Nook.

"Homework," she said as she walked past him and breathed in. She loved the smell of Book Nook. It always smelled like a combination of leather, furniture polish, and old books. The large store had dark wood shelves, big leather chairs and couches that were perfect for sinking into with a good book, and, in the back, a row of heavy wood tables with old brass desk lamps. Ginny walked to the table on the far right of the store, the one with the least visibility, and set down her backpack and hot chocolate. This was where she spent nearly every Sunday morning. Ginny and her dad used to spend hours here, finding new books and reading— or Dad worked and Ginny did homework. It was their place until the divorce.

"Thanks for bringing me a coffee," Pete joked as he walked between the tables to the stock room. He was always sarcastic with Ginny, which she loved. He was like the older brother she'd never had and he took her mind off of the fact that every time she was there, the void of Dad's absence felt even bigger. If that was possible.

"Anytime." She emptied her backpack and settled into the wood and leather desk chair. She'd remained calm all morning as she went through her regular Sunday routine, but as she opened her laptop, it was as if she'd set free hundreds of fluttering butterflies in her stomach. As soon as she was connected to Wi-Fi, the Chatter window opened up on the lower left hand side of her screen.

Sportstatsguy: Hey you.

Ginny smiled and sat up. Sportstatsguy was the username of Mitch Henry, and he said this nearly every morning even though they'd never actually met. Or at least he didn't know that they had. She loved the way he talked to her even though they only shared an online friendship. Or relationship. She didn't know what it was. Her hands were poised above the backlit silver keyboard as she wondered how she should respond. She had to act normal. She set her hands down and started typing her usual response.

Rosco: Hey you. How'd you sleep? What are you doing today?

She stopped typing, cursor blinking, and thought about the potential directions in which the conversation could go. She needed to get to work and couldn't be distracted. She deleted what she'd typed and started over.

Rosco: Hey you. I'm working on a big project today. Talk later?

She hit send and waited to see if Mitch would write back. Ginny's screen name was Rosco, the name her dad had called her since she was little. It was a character from a show he watched when he was a kid. She sat back in her chair and took a drink of her hot chocolate. The whipped cream had melted into the drink, making it frothy and creamy. She shut her eyes momentarily as she took another sip, and when she opened them she saw a new message.

Sportstatsguy: Band concert this afternoon, show at 7pm, otherwise I'll be around. Good luck with your project!

She laughed nervously and closed out the chat. She longed to keep talking to him but she didn't trust herself not to say something she shouldn't. And it was time to get to work. She opened an audio file called JakeSophiaCall. She pushed play, as she had dozens of times, and listened to the first few words. Then she fast-forwarded to the end of the file to hear the last ten seconds.

"Really? Seriously?" a boy's voice asked.

"I think it would be really . . ." a girl's voice started, ". . . amazing."

"Still there . . ." Ginny said quietly, smiling to herself. Looking up from the computer, she took the muffin and a glasses case out of her backpack. She put the glasses on top of her head and carefully tore off the top of the muffin, the best part as far as she was concerned. She broke a small piece and popped it into her mouth, her attention returning to the screen.

Next, she selected a second audio file called TheWholeTruth. Once again, she listened to the first and last few seconds of the clip, confirming that the audio files were the same as they were when she last checked.

The files were ready. All that remained was programming the hack.

Ginny double-clicked on the image of a masked burglar's face peeking from behind an MP3 player. As the software loaded, she stood from her chair and looked in both directions and toward the front of the shop. It appeared that she was still the lone customer at Book Nook. She walked to a place where she could see the front counter. Pete was busy with something on his computer. Satisfied that she was safe from prying eyes, she returned to her seat. She opened the file called JakeSophiaHack, and a green window opened revealing a full page of code. Ginny looked up from her screen again, taking a sip of her hot chocolate. When she returned her gaze to her screen, she pulled her glasses down on her nose and began quickly reviewing the hack.

Ginny had practiced this several times already. Ever since Mitch mentioned last week that he wished he could get more listeners for his podcast. She knew the hack would work, but she had to be sure it was perfect. For Mitch. When she was done looking over all of the code, she looked up again. Pete was coming toward her with an armful of books. Ginny froze. She couldn't slam her laptop shut without looking suspicious, but the hacking software she was using was, technically, illegal. She was sure Pete wouldn't have a clue what she was doing, but what if he somehow figured it out? She quickly minimized the PodHack window and maximized the internet window and pushed play.

"What's that?" he asked, nodding toward her laptop.

"Hmm?" Ginny tried to appear as though she was completely engrossed in the YouTube video that played on her screen.

"That," he said.

"Oh, this is a cheerleading competition that happened last summer in Texas. These teams are really good and I'm trying to figure out if we can incorporate any of their stunts into what we do."

Pete snorted.

"That's the project you're working on?"

"Umm . . . yeah? What's wrong with it?" Ginny was irritated that he was mocking her. She did, in fact, watch YouTube videos of cheer competitions. Not often, but they sometimes gave her ideas for the eighth grade squad.

"Nothing!" Pete made his way back to the stockroom. "Sounds riveting!" he said, as the door swung shut behind him.

Ginny shook her head. He really was just like an older brother. She turned back to her screen and watched a small girl get tossed into the air by two male cheerleaders, her long ponytail flying behind her as she spun. She had to keep watching until Pete went back up front. He finally emerged from the stockroom, smiling, and yelling, "Be aggressive! B-E-AGG-RESS-IVE!" Ginny scowled at him, more for show than in actual annoyance, and minimized the YouTube video as soon as he was out of sight.

Once PodHack was open again, Ginny clicked the "Schedule" button. This brought up a window where she could choose the target and timing of the hack. From a dropdown menu she chose "SportswithMitch." Then she went to the dropdown menu for time and scrolled to 7:07 p.m. She checked and unchecked a couple of boxes in the window and then looked at every selection carefully.

Ginny took a deep breath and sat back. She finished her muffin and washed it down with hot chocolate. The time on the top right of her screen said 10:40 a.m. All she had to do was hit "Submit" and the plan would be underway. She chewed the inside of her cheek, something she did when she was anxious, and sat up. The butterflies in her stomach multiplied and adrenaline kicked in. She wasn't sure what she'd do with all of this nervous energy until 7:07 p.m. She moved the mouse to the "Submit" button, hesitating just briefly, and clicked. A small window popped up with the masked burglar giving Ginny a thumbs up. Under his picture it said, "Congratulations! Your hacking will be done!" She quickly closed out the window and slammed her laptop shut. She sat, looking around, brimming with excitement. She wished she could tell her friends. She almost wished she could tell Mitch. But she'd have to keep the secret to herself for the plan to work.

2

MITCH

The letter arrived more than a week ago. Usually envelopes from Podder held coupons for more sophisticated services, ads for upcoming podcast events, and flyers announcing upgrades to products. All things that Mitch Henry promptly threw into recycling. That's why the letter sat in a pile on Mitch's desk for several days before he opened it.

When he finally did, he knew it was a different kind of letter when he saw the words "we regret to inform you" at the top of the page. He'd fallen into his desk chair and read the rest as a lump formed in his throat. He didn't have enough listeners for PodderSports and their advertisers to keep him on their list of "Best Amateur Sports Podcasts." Mitch had until October 5th to significantly increase his number of listeners, or he'd lose his place, the ability to call for free technical help, and any advertisers that Podder had directed to his show. Unless he was willing to pay a hefty fee each month to keep it going. It would be the end of *Sports with Mitch*.

He'd read the letter three times and was on the verge of tears when Rosco messaged him on Chatter.

Rosco: Hey you…
Sportstatsguy: Hey you…just got bad news. :(
Rosco: ???
Sportstatsguy: Podder is going to bump me from Podder-SportsNetwork unless I get like eighty more listeners for every show or start paying.
Rosco: Noooooo!!! But only eighty listeners? You could get that. Your show is awesome!

Mitch's smile was sad. What Rosco didn't know was that the most listeners he'd ever actually had for one show was twenty. When he started, he thought he'd for sure get all the guys he used to go to school with. He'd been surprised when most of his listeners were athletes from the high school. Guys who didn't even know who he was but liked hearing about local sports in addition to what was going on nationally. Eighty listeners could have been 600 as far as Mitch was concerned.

Sportstatsguy: It's ok, I'll figure something out. What's new with u?

He knew she'd keep trying to help but he had to somehow fix this himself. The podcast was his way of participating in sports even though he couldn't play anymore. It kept him involved and he *needed* that. He needed that so bad. And that meant he needed money. While he waited for Rosco to respond, he opened his desk drawer and pulled out a notebook that held all of the information for his lawn-mowing and snow-shoveling business. He started doing the math on how many more clients he needed to be able to afford the Podder payments.

> Rosco: *Sorry. Getting ready to head home. G'ma Weber is still there.*
> Sportstatsguy: *Ha! THAT will be fun.*
> Rosco: *Umm. Yeah. What will you do about your podcast?*

Mitch felt his throat tighten again. What would he do? He couldn't lose it. He simply couldn't.

> Sportstatsguy: *Probably rob a bank to cover the fees. I am sure I won't get caught.*
> Rosco: *Do you want help? I can run really fast and jump really high (not sure how that helps but it might).*
> Sportstatsguy: *Let's do it. G2G. Thx for cheering me up.*
> Rosco: *That is what I'm here for silly. Later.*
> Sportstatsguy: *Later.*

She was his closest friend. Which, he knew, was weird. Not only was she a girl, but he hadn't ever actually met her in person. When his mom decided to keep him home for school, she was looking for creative ways to keep him challenged. She found a study that a well-respected university was doing on children and computer programming. She applied, and Mitch got in. He and seven other kids from across the country met three times per week, online, and learned computer programming and coding. One of the rules they had to follow was not to reveal their real names, locations, or anything that would allow the kids to find each other in real life. It had something to do with the study, and the anonymity of the kids involved, all of whom were much younger than eighteen. The leader of the study, and Mitch's parents, had been very clear that this was a rule that was not to be broken.

In the first week he was partnered with Rosco. For the first month he thought she was a boy. Rosco sounded like a boy's screen name, after all. Usually girls picked screen names that made it obvious they were girls. Things like QTPIE227 (his sister Addie's) or PRTYNPNK43 or GRLYGRL179. Then she told him one day that she had to go because she and her mom were going dress shopping for a wedding.

"I hate when my mom drags me shopping with her. I only like shopping when it's for me." Mitch had said.

"No, it's for me. I'm a junior bridesmaid in my cousin's wedding. We're going to find MY dress."

Mitch didn't even know how to respond. He gave an excuse to get offline and spent the weekend trying to figure out how he'd been so wrong. By then they'd partnered on several projects, they'd played Steep on Xbox a few times, and they'd become friends. After two days of not really talking, he got on his Xbox to play and she was online. They started playing and trash-talking like they normally did, and Mitch decided her being a girl didn't really matter.

■ ■ ■

Mitch climbed into the backseat of his dad's big sedan next to his ten-year-old sister, Addie, who was looking at her phone and giggling. He leaned closer to see what was so funny. A red fox and a small spotted puppy were playing in a large snow-covered yard. Addie's giggles turned into loud belly laughs as the furry animals tumbled around in the snow.

"How do you even find these things?" Mitch felt a little annoyed at her giddiness when he was about to lose something that meant so much to him.

"People send them to me," Addie responded cheerfully. Mitch shook his head as if it were ridiculous but continued watching the video.

"Turn the sound off, please," Mom said as she got into the passenger seat. The scent of her perfume and hair products filled the car. She always smelled spicy and clean.

"Who's ready for today?" Dad bellowed, getting into the front seat and starting the car. As he pulled out of the garage, Mitch heard him whisper, "Is it ready?" His mom nodded and smiled mischievously.

"Okay, I think you know what song we have to listen to," Dad said as he turned right onto the busy road that would bring them to Main Street and Book Nook. "We have to get you pumped for your first school band concert of the year, buddy!" Addie put her phone down in anticipation and Mitch rolled his eyes. He looked at the car beside them to see if it held anyone he recognized. He knew what was coming and didn't want to be seen by any of his classmates. They already thought he was weird.

The music was fast and loud. It was from an old movie his parents loved. In the movie, the song played during a karate tournament as the main character won match after match. His parents played it on the way to every major event that Addie and Mitch participated in. His parents and Addie danced, jostling the entire car, karate chopping at certain lyrics.

"You're the best (chop), around, nothing's gonna ever keep you down," they all sang at the top of their lungs. Mitch tried to keep from smiling, he was sulking after all, but secretly he loved this tradition.

"Come on Mitchell, you need to prepare for your concert, let's go!" his mom prodded from the front seat. After another quick glance at the cars driving in the other lane, Mitch joined them, karate chops and all. By the time they pulled into the parking lot, they'd listened to the song three times, and Mitch really did feel pumped up for his concert. They walked to the book store, his parents holding hands and his mom still humming. His sister bounced behind them and randomly karate-chopped the crisp fall air. Mitch trailed behind carrying his saxophone case, music book, and stand.

They weren't often all together. His dad worked a lot, his mom was in law school, and both he and Addie had activities. Usually his parents had to "divide and conquer" to make sure everyone was where they had to be, and they were always in a hurry. But when they were together, Mitch was reminded that his parents were crazy about each other and they all had so much fun as a family.

Mr. Swan pointed at each kid who walked through the heavy wood and glass doors and then at the spot where he wanted them to set-up. There were six other kids already playing a chaotic mix of songs and sounds. It was a little like geese honking. They'd only been playing together for a few weeks, but each fall and spring, Book Nook gave a percentage of their sales to the Kenwood band program and the band had to perform for shoppers. Mr. Swan hand-picked the group that would play today from the classes he taught at the junior and senior high schools. Even though Mitch started playing sax a couple of years ago, he was still shocked to be one of the few junior high kids that were chosen. He didn't want to screw this up.

They stood in a half circle in front of a large book display in matching dark pants and white shirts. Mr. Swan stood in the middle facing them in red skinny jeans and suspenders, his long hair in a bun on the top of his head. As they started the first song, "When the Saints Go Marching In," Mitch saw that both his parents, and Addie, had their phones poised to take pictures or videos. Mom and Dad were beaming, and even Addie seemed excited. He returned his focus to his music book and played as carefully as he could. When they finished the song, the shoppers and parents of the other musicians gave a loud round of applause. He breathed a sigh of relief. He was able to keep up with everyone and was feeling more confident.

"Nice job, dude," said the high school sax player that stood next to him. Mitch nodded his thanks but could barely contain his relief and pride. Not only was this guy a saxophone player, but he also played baseball for the high school. Mitch had not only seen him play, but talked about his games on *Sports with Mitch* many times.

At that moment Mitch knew that losing the podcast was not an option. He would find a way to get more listeners, or to pay for it, but either way, *Sports with Mitch* would continue no matter what he had to do. He put his lips on the bite plate of his sax's mouthpiece, ready to start playing "Low Rider," and stood a little taller.

3

GINNY

Ginny's Grandma Weber was not like normal grandmothers. She didn't bake cookies or take Ginny shopping. She didn't have the warmth that most grandmothers do. When Ginny hugged her, which was rare, she didn't feel safe and protected like she imagined her friends did when they hugged their grandmothers. It always felt awkward and forced. Grandma Weber was more like Dr. Jekyll and Mr. Hyde. Ginny was never sure if she'd be nice or frosty.

Things had gotten worse since Grandma's back had started acting up again. Mom said she was in pain "most of the time," which Ginny couldn't even imagine. But it meant that her frosty streaks lasted longer than they used to and the times when she was warm and kind were few and far between.

She peeked into the kitchen and saw Grandma sitting in the sunny breakfast nook. She was wearing a matching green argyle sweater and golf pants, and reading the paper. Ginny breathed in the strong smell of coffee that filled the entire first floor of her house. It reminded her of Dad. Mom didn't drink coffee, so Ginny hardly ever smelled it anymore except for when Grandma stayed with her. Since her parents had divorced, Grandma had become the regular babysitter and it always made Ginny miss her dad even more than usual. She shrugged out of her backpack, took a deep breath, and walked into the kitchen.

"It smells good in here," Ginny said, a little timidly. Grandma looked up from her newspaper, a brief wince of pain barely visible under the green golf visor that held her silver hair in place. She had beautiful hair that fell straight on both sides of her face and curled under at the bottom. It looked perfect all the time.

"I was at the bookstore working on a project," Ginny continued, half wishing she'd just gone straight upstairs instead of stopping in the kitchen.

"I have a tee time in half an hour, and then cards with the girls, so I won't be back today. Your mother should be home around dinner time. You can manage until then?" Grandma raised her right eyebrow in question. Ginny wondered, for a second, what Grandma would say if she said she couldn't. Sometimes Ginny thought Grandma forgot that she was only thirteen years old. But today, Ginny was grateful for the independence.

"Yep," Ginny answered. "I can call you if I need anything?"

"Mmm hmm," she said nodding, already returning her attention to the paper. "Have a good day, Ginny." She lifted her right hand in a sort of wave, or possibly a dismissal, and Ginny turned for her bedroom. When she was halfway up the stairs, she heard Grandma quietly call out, "Love you."

■ ■ ■

The day felt like it both lasted a lifetime and went by in a flash. Ginny stood in front of the microwave watching the bag of popcorn twitch and expand. She didn't think her nervous stomach could handle a larger dinner, and since her mom's flight was delayed, there was nobody home to encourage her to eat a better meal. Focused on her popcorn, she was startled when the microwave beeped and accidentally backed up into a sleeping Lucky. Ginny squeaked and stepped forward, apologizing to the golden retriever with a scratch behind his soft yellow ears. Bowl of popcorn and soda in hand, Lucky at her heels, she turned off the kitchen light and made her way through the empty house to her bedroom.

Ginny settled into the bright blue chair in front of her white wooden desk. She set her bowl of popcorn and soda next to her laptop and opened it. When the screen lit up, the clock on the upper-right-hand corner read 6:58. It was just about time. She logged into Chatter and wrote a quick message.

Rosco: Have a good show.

Mitch was quick to respond.

Sportstatsguy: FOOTBALL!!!

Ginny smiled. Mitch's love of sports was one of the many things she liked about him. It reminded Ginny of her dad. She missed Sundays when he still lived at home. The sound of football games, along with her father yelling at the TV, and the smell of chili filling the large house. That's one of the reasons she started listening to Mitch's show in the first place. To simply hear sports on Sundays again. Now she listened to every show because she liked Mitch. So much.

She sat back, watching the clock on her screen, absently stuffing popcorn in her mouth. At 7 p.m. drums and trumpets signaled the beginning of the state university's marching band playing the school song. Mitch played it at the beginning of every show. Ginny could feel her heart beating fast, and it felt like the hundreds of butterflies in her stomach were doing flips. She giggled and rubbed her sweaty palms on her flannel pajama bottoms.

"You've tuned in to another Sunday edition of *Sports with Mitch*. We have a lot to talk about tonight, with the opening of the NFL season. We also have to talk about this weekend's high school and college games. Did you see the U's defense? Before we start, and before I take calls, here's the best clip of the weekend. The Steelers' press conference with Coach Tomlin. I know you've all heard it by now, but it deserves to be heard again."

She quickly opened KenChat, her school district's unofficial social media site. It wasn't likely that her friends would even be listening to the show. They didn't care about sports, and they were just starting to remember Mitch. Older brothers listened, though, and maybe some of her friends would overhear it from their computers. She had both chat windows open, side by side, ready to react to whatever came up first. If anything.

Ginny returned her focus to the clip, the Coach was yelling at a reporter, something about the shame of focusing on the "shenanigans" of his players instead of their actual play on the field. The clock read 7:07. She sat up straight, took a sip of soda, and opened a third window. This one housed an app that allowed people to text from "unknown" numbers. She typed out a text and sat back in her chair. She'd send it when it was time.

"It's laughable to think that we're just supposed to—" Mitch was saying when he was cut off and the sound of static replaced his voice. Ginny's eyes widened. This was it. She reached to turn the volume up and realized her damp hands were now shaking. Just as suddenly as Mitch had been interrupted by static, the static stopped, and Ginny heard her own voice. It was several octaves lower than her actual voice, but it was her alright. The program she'd hacked earlier had taken over. Any listeners of Mitch's show were now listening to her show.

"Welcome to *The Whole Truth*," a tinny and automated sounding voice announced.

Ginny stepped up from her chair abruptly and started to pace along the edges of her room. Lucky looked up from his place at the end of her bed and watched her. She stopped to rub his belly but started walking again when she heard someone speaking.

"Can we talk about something serious?" It was a boy's voice. Ginny wasn't sure if anyone would recognize it as Jake

Dietrich, one of Kenwood High School's most well-liked football players, but they'd know he was a teenager.

"That doesn't sound good," replied a girl. The voice was familiar, like it could have been any one of her friends. Ginny was glad about that. She wanted people to wonder if it was someone they knew. This voice was that of Sophia Von Ulm. She was one of the nicest girls Ginny knew from the high school. She was captain of the synchronized swimming team and a cheerleader in the fall. Ginny had met her at tryouts for the JV squad last spring. Sophia supervised fall practices, so Ginny saw her a couple of times each week. Even though Ginny was still in junior high, Sophia treated her like just another high school cheerleader.

"No, nothing bad," Jake assured her.

"Okay?" Sophia sounded nervous.

"Do you want to go to Homecoming with me?" Jake's words tumbled out quickly. Ginny's heart fluttered. She and her friends always talked about what it would be like to be asked to Homecoming. She loved this phone call because it was real and she hoped someday she would have the same conversation with Mitch.

"Sure. Who else should we ask?" Sophia's voice had returned to normal. She sounded casual. Not as excited as Ginny would be if Mitch asked her to the dance.

"No. I mean, I want *us* to go together."

"Right. I'm saying who should we ask to come with us?" Sophia almost seemed distracted, like she was doing something else. Ginny imagined her looking at the cheerleading schedule for the week, or working on homework.

"I mean," there was a long pause, "not as friends," Jake continued quietly. It had almost been hard to hear, but that's what made this clip so sweet. This popular guy was nervous and shy about asking Sophia to the dance. "I'm wondering if we can go together . . . as more than friends," he said.

There was another long pause. Ginny wondered what Mitch must be thinking and doing. Probably frantically trying to figure out how his show had been interrupted and how to get back on the air.

When Ginny first got ahold of this phone call, it had been like watching a movie. She'd never gone to a dance—this was the first year she was old enough to go. Jake and Sophia were seniors in high school, and it was so romantic. She'd wanted to have all of her friends listen to it, but, of course, that would have ruined the plan.

"It's okay," he was talking quickly again, trying to fill the silence. "We can stay just friends. I just thought I'd ask."

"I would love to." This was almost a whisper and Ginny sucked in a gulp of air. She'd been holding her breath. "I mean," Sophia continued, "as more than friends."

This time the sound of air being sucked in came from Jake. He gasped.

"Really? Seriously?" He sounded relieved, elated, but most of all, shocked.

"I think it would be really"—Sophia paused again, and this time her voice was louder and more confident—"amazing."

For a second, as she sat on her bed with a hand resting on Lucky's soft yellow back, Ginny was caught up in the call. If her plan worked, she might be having this same conversation with

Mitch in a few weeks. He'd finally know who she really was, and his podcast would be saved. She squealed at the thought of it, stomping her feet on her plush carpeted floor. If she could go to Homecoming with Mitch, and save his podcast, the risks she was taking would be worth it.

At the return of her own voice coming through her laptop speakers, Ginny jumped up from her bed and took three large steps to her desk. It was the end of the segment and the end of the interruption to Mitch's show.

"Join us Tuesday for more of *The Whole Truth*," her lower voice said. Then the static returned briefly.

She hit send on the text she'd written before the hack took over Mitch's show and listened as the static receded to dead air.

Unknown Number, 7:11pm: You should probably congratulate the happy couple before you go back to talking about football.

4

MITCH

Mitch looked at the athletic fields behind the junior high school through the blinds covering his bedroom windows. It was late Sunday night, and nearly all of the fields were still packed. Half of them were filled with men's soccer leagues, while the other half held little kid bodies topped with football shoulder pads and helmets that looked disproportionately large. Mitch sighed. He wasn't that much older than many of the kids out there when he stopped playing football. And now, not only would he be losing his podcast, but it appeared someone was hacking into it.

It didn't make sense. He barely had any listeners. Why would any hacker waste time on his podcast? He could understand if it were popular, but he talked about sports, even junior high games; it's not like his was a well-known show. So why? And what would Podder do if they found out about it? He didn't think that they paid much attention to anything but numbers of listeners, but what if they also monitored content?

Panic started rising, and he could feel his heart beating faster. He turned his focus back to the kids playing football.

"Enjoy it while it lasts," Mitch said, taking a gulp of Mountain Dew.

"What's that?" Mitch spun around to see his mom coming into his bedroom with a basket of folded clothes.

"Nothing," Mitch took the basket and set it on the floor next to his dresser.

"How was your show tonight?" Mom asked, sitting down on Mitch's bed. She looked tired, her black hair piled messily on top of her head, and she'd taken her make-up off.

Mitch focused on the shirts he was putting away. He did not want to involve his parents in whatever was going on. "Great," he lied. "How's school?" He wanted to change the subject. He stood up and put the now-empty laundry basket on the floor by her feet and sat across from her at his desk.

She smiled. "I just keep telling myself, 'It's the last year, it's the last year, it's the last year.'" She was wearing leggings, one of his dad's old sweatshirts, and moccasins. She didn't look as old as she was. He guessed that her classmates didn't even know she was that much older than they were. She'd started law school a few months after she quit her job to homeschool Mitch, after the accident that ended his football career. If you can call it a "football career" when you have to stop playing in sixth grade.

"How's being back at school?" she asked.

Mitch leaned back in his chair and thought about the question. "It's all right. The schoolwork is easier than it was when you were my teacher." This made her laugh out loud. He loved it when his mother laughed. She stopped and leaned closer to him.

"What about friends? Is that going okay?" Mitch knew his parents were worried about this. Her concern made her look even more tired. He could see the lines that were starting to deepen around her eyes more clearly than usual.

"I mean . . ." Mitch started. The truth was, it wasn't as easy as he thought it would be. Some people thought he was weird because he had been home-schooled for the majority of the past two years. His closest friend from before, Josh Weinberg, was coming around slowly. Mitch had all but fallen off the face of the earth after the accident because of how long it took his injuries to heal. Mom had been so worried and over-protective, she hadn't spent a lot of time focusing on the state of his friendships. And when you're in sixth grade, your social life is pretty much dependent upon your parents.

"Josh is cool. I have a couple of classes with him. Most of my friends still play sports together, so . . ." Mitch trailed off. His mom's expression tightened.

"Well, I'm sure after another couple of weeks, it will be like you were never gone. Don't you think?" She got up, and Mitch knew the conversation was coming to an end.

Mitch looked up at her. "Yep."

"I know it will," she said as she leaned toward him. She pushed back his curly hair and kissed his forehead, her spicy soapy smell filling his nose. "Your dad will be up shortly. He's finishing up his closing argument for tomorrow." She grabbed the empty basket and left Mitch alone in his room.

Mitch shut down his computer and started getting ready for bed. He walked back into his room after brushing his teeth and heard his text alert. He picked up his phone and, to his surprise, there was a message from Josh.

Josh Weinberg, 8:47pm: Heard the show. Wha??? Tell me about it tomorrow.

Mitch's stomach dropped. Josh hadn't texted him in he didn't know how long. It also meant Josh listened to his podcast. Mitch didn't know if he did regularly, but he did tonight. Mitch felt embarrassed that Josh had heard the debacle that was tonight's show. It was a disaster. He typed a message and sent it.

Mitch Henry, 8:49pm: I know, right?

Mitch went downstairs to say good night to his dad and wondered if his mom was right. Maybe in a few weeks it really would feel like he'd never left school. That would be good, but would he still have his podcast in a few weeks? The thought caused his chest to tighten. It would be great to have his friends again, obviously, but he couldn't bear the thought of losing *Sports with Mitch.*

■ ■ ■

Mitch listened to ESPN radio and inhaled a bagel with cream cheese as he cut across the athletic fields to the back entrance of the junior high. He stomped his feet on the rubber mat inside the doors to shake off the morning dew his shoes had soaked up from the grass. He nodded at a couple of sixth graders and yanked the earbuds out of his ears so they hung around his neck. As he neared his locker, he saw Josh Weinberg coming from the opposite direction. He braced himself. He had no idea what Josh would think about the hack and wasn't sure he wanted to.

"What's up?" Josh asked, shifting his books from one arm to the other.

"Hey," Mitch said, turning the combination lock and opening his locker door. He pulled off his fleece jacket, his flannel shirt getting stuck in the sleeve. He dropped his backpack and untangled himself, stuffing the fleece in the top shelf.

"So was that thing planned last night?" Josh leaned against the wall while Mitch searched for his first-hour notebook.

Mitch shook his head, both in confusion and frustration. The hacker had turned *his* show into something else completely. "I don't know what that was." As Mitch said this, Tyler Humphrey, Jin Zhao, and Zach Jameson joined them.

"Oh, I thought that was part of the show," Zach said.

Mitch looked at him skeptically. "Umm, no. You were listening?"

"My brother and I always listen when we're working out." Zach responded like this would be obvious, but Mitch was shocked. He didn't know any of these guys even knew he had a podcast.

"Oh. Yeah, well no," Mitch said, embarrassed.

"What do you think about the U playing Coleman?" Jin asked the group. "I mean, *Zach* is a better quarterback," he joked. And just like that, they were talking about sports. It was the first time since school started that he felt like his childhood friends remembered who he actually was. They hadn't been unkind, they just didn't really talk to him other than a nod or a "hey" when they saw him. Mitch had been away from school for only two years, but it was like they hardly knew him even though they'd gone to school together since kindergarten. Now they were acting like he'd never left.

They continued to talk about sports as the five-minute bell rang. In the short time they stood by Mitch's locker, they covered college football and the NFL, and the guys even asked a couple of questions about the mysterious phone call that hijacked his podcast the night before.

Mitch hadn't realized how lonely he'd been for the past two weeks. He looked up, away from the group, and saw Robin Blair walking down the hall alone. Usually she was with Ginny Ross, and Mitch wondered where she was. He liked Ginny and Robin, especially Ginny. She was smart and had always been funny. Robin was cool and nice too, and something was going on with her and Josh. Mitch's heart, though, was tangled up with Rosco. He wished he could see *her* in the halls every day.

"Spanish?" Jin asked Mitch. Mitch nodded and slammed his locker shut.

"Later," he said over his shoulder as he and Jin walked in the opposite direction of Josh, Tyler, and Zach.

■ ■ ■

Mitch stared blankly at his iPad in third-hour Life Science. He was supposed to be researching a recent science related "happening" that he could present to the class next week, but he couldn't concentrate. When the screen went dark, he tapped it and an article about the next super moon came up. He continued to do this without thinking as the minutes went by. He knew the guys only came to his locker that morning because Josh was standing there. While he knew that was true, it seemed to change the dynamic between them all. He didn't feel like such an outsider anymore.

"Mitchell?" asked Ms. Getty. She was standing next to him and looking down at his sleeping iPad. "Are you," she paused, "thinking about how to proceed?"

Mitch looked up and tapped the screen. "Yes, just thinking about how to present this topic."

Ms. Getty smiled and nodded. She knew he'd been day-dreaming. "Good," she said as she continued up the aisle of desks.

Mitch started reading the article. He was only a few sentences in when someone tapped his shoulder from behind. He was turning around when a folded note was shoved over his shoulder by Lily, who sat behind him. He took it and quickly put it in his lap to unfold. Ms. Getty didn't put up with any nonsense and he liked her. He positioned his iPad to cover the note, just in case she came back down his aisle.

I didn't know you had your own podcast. That's so cool!
—Becca

Mitch wrinkled his nose. He crumpled the note and stuffed it into his jeans pocket. He pretended to return his attention to the assignment but his mind spun. Becca. Becca?! She was the only person that knew him since kindergarten who was blatantly rude to him when he came back to school this year. She told people stories about why he left school in sixth grade, none of which were true. He overheard her call him a weirdo under her breath when he passed her once in the media center. Mitch knew he wasn't special: Becca wasn't really nice to anyone. But now she was sending him notes? And she knew he had a podcast too. When he found out he needed more listeners, he definitely hadn't hoped for listeners like Becca who couldn't care less about the sports he talked about. He went back to pretending to read about the super moon while trying to make sense of this crazy day.

5

GINNY

Ginny was wary as she walked into Kenwood Junior High School on Monday. A morning dentist appointment kept her from hearing any gossip that may have spread in the first couple of hours of school. Her mom came home late the night before, long after Ginny was in bed, and had been chatty all morning, wanting to "catch up." She hadn't even been able to text with Robin or her other friends because they were all in class. She was heading into school blind on the gossip front.

She reached her locker just as Robin Blair was about to close it.

"Hey, Gin," Robin swung the door open again and started on the combination for the one next to it. Robin, her best friend since fourth grade, had nicely asked the boy who used to have the locker next to Ginny's to trade at the beginning of seventh grade. It was too hard to grab books and find each other between classes when they were on opposite sides of the building. Ginny cleared out her backpack and stuffed the empty bag into the bare locker that held their jackets and bags. Robin shut the metal door and leaned on it while Ginny rummaged through the notebooks. This locker had walls of light blue with tiny silver dots, a small silver chandelier that turned on when the door was open, a mirror, a variety of beauty products on the top shelf, and, in the large bottom portion, white wire shelves to hold their books, calculators, and iPads.

"How was Grandma this weekend? Did you guys bond?" Robin smiled wickedly. Ginny glanced at the hallway behind her through the reflection in the mirror. The hall was bustling with activity, but there was nothing out of the ordinary and she hadn't heard anyone mention Mitch, his podcast, or the interruption of Jake and Sophia's call.

"Yes. Lots of quality time with Grandma between her golf and her card games," Ginny said. She pressed her lips together, spreading shimmery gloss back and forth across them. "Come on, let's go to lunch." She shut the locker door gingerly. They'd quickly learned that slamming the door caused the fragile chandelier to fall and break into a million pieces. Three broken chandeliers, and four very irritated parents later, they'd adjusted to being much more careful when closing the metal door.

They walked down the hall, saying "hi" to nearly everyone, and turned into the cafeteria. Ginny's eyes automatically went to the eighth grade lunch tables. Mitch usually sat by himself listening to headphones. Today, however, instead of seeing him eating and reading his phone, she saw him standing in a small huddle of guys. Robin was talking about the student council elections, but Ginny was straining to catch any of the things being said in the group as they drew closer.

" . . . about Coleman? You can hardly call him a quarter-back. You don't think they'll play him on Satur—"

" . . . Steelers have nothin' on the Colts. You have to be kidding . . ."

Ginny couldn't identify who was saying what, but as she and Robin strode past the table, she could see on Mitch's face that he was enjoying himself. Robin waved at Josh and smiled. His whole face lit up and he waved back. Mitch looked up, and Ginny averted her eyes using her left hand to flip her thick, wavy hair over her shoulder.

"You guys should listen tomorrow night and call in . . ." she heard him saying as she and Robin got to the lunch line. They greeted the seventh grade girls that were standing at the end of the line, and Ginny snuck a look back at Mitch and the other guys. If what she just saw was any indication, her plan would work. Soon enough, she might be standing with Mitch in the middle of an even bigger group of people. As his girlfriend.

■ ■ ■

"I think it's Samantha, you know, that ninth grade volleyball player with black hair?" Emily Whittaker was saying loudly as Ginny sat down next to her at their lunch table. Eighth graders sat by the window-filled back wall of the cafeteria. It offered views of the many athletic fields behind the school and, coincidentally, Mitch's house.

Robin set her tray across the table from Ginny and shaded her eyes from the sun streaming in. "Play it again," she said.

"I've only heard it once." In the bright sunlight, hints of dark auburn peeked out of Robin's long black hair and her skin looked like bronze.

"I want to hear it too," Ginny said between bites of her rib sandwich. Her body was buzzing with excitement, and more than once she had to stop herself from bouncing her knees and shaking the entire table. She'd feigned ignorance in the lunch line when Robin explained what she'd heard from their classmates. Now she focused on her sandwich and keeping her legs still, in an attempt to seem only a little interested.

Emily pulled her yellow phone from the front pocket of her Kenwood Soccer hoodie and set it in the middle of the table. She tapped the screen three times and adjusted the volume on the side. The four girls stopped eating, lowered their heads, and leaned their ears toward the phone so they could hear.

As they listened to Mitch's podcast from the night before, Ginny snuck glimpses of her friends, careful not to let them see she was watching them. Excitement, curiosity, and awe-filled expressions showed on their faces. When Mitch came back on and congratulated the couple, Emily stopped the podcast and returned the phone to her sweatshirt pocket. For a moment, they sat silent, looking at one another.

Alicia Davis tucked her brown hair behind her ears and broke the silence. "There is no way that's Samantha," she said definitively. "I've been going to synagogue with her since I was five, and that's not what she sounds like."

"I wonder what Mitch says about it," Emily said, nodding her curly red head in the direction of the eighth grade boys who sat at the other end of their table. Ginny, Robin, and Alicia followed her gaze and saw Mitch sitting with Josh, Tyler, Zach, and Jin. Athletes. Josh was telling a story, using his hands as he talked while the others laughed. Ginny sucked her chocolate milk through a straw, eyes wide as she watched them.

"I wonder what people are saying at the high school," Robin said, through a mouthful of yellow cake. The girls turned to Emily expectantly.

Emily rolled her eyes. "I'll try to find out tonight from my brother. He doesn't really pay attention . . . to anything . . . so I might not get much out of him, but I'll try." They laughed.

Ginny thought about Emily's brother Grant. A star hockey player, he might listen to Mitch's show, but he wasn't the kind of guy to keep up on the gossip of the high school. The girls often tried to get Grant to give them insider information on his cute teammates when they were over at Emily's house. What he knew about them, or any other important high school gossip, was surprisingly little. Grant likely wouldn't have much to offer on the aftermath of last night's call.

Ginny reached into her back jeans pocket for her phone. "Let's see what people on KenChat are saying," she said, but quickly realized that the phone wasn't there. She checked her other pockets and, after coming up empty, looked up at her friends with worry.

"Locker. Last time I saw you with it was when you were walking into school," said Robin. "I'll go with you."

Ginny stood, sighing as she grabbed her lunch tray. She was relieved to be getting up—it had been difficult to keep her mouth shut as they talked about Mitch's show. She waved to

Alicia and Emily as she and Robin returned their lunch trays before going in search of her phone.

As they walked, Robin relayed what Ginny had missed in Advisory that morning and Ginny's mind wandered. Her friends knew she talked to a boy online. She told them a few weeks after she and Mitch "met," not able to hide her excitement. They'd been online friends for more than a year when, this past summer, she realized that Sportstatsguy was *Mitch Henry*.

His disappearance from school a couple of years earlier was the subject of wild rumors that circulated for months. Even though teachers explained that he'd been hit by a car while riding his bike, kids came up with alternate stories that were much more exciting. Some people said he was moving to Hollywood to become a movie star. Others said his parents were running from the FBI and had to leave suddenly so they wouldn't get caught. Becca Bills, a mean but popular girl that Ginny and her friends tried to avoid, made up the most popular theory. Mitch's family was in a cult and they decided to homeschool him so he'd be ready to take over cult leadership someday. The rumors had fizzled but resurfaced when Mitch showed up at the beginning of this school year.

Ginny was listening to the show in August, and Sportstatsguy started talking about going back to school at Kenwood. Of course, Ginny knew her online friend had a podcast and he talked about college, professional, and sometimes high school sports, but she paid so little attention to the actual details of what he was talking about. She'd figured out her friend's name was Mitch from his show, but she never thought he was Mitch Henry that she grew up with. Her attention was piqued when he said he was going back to Kenwood, and she started listening more intently. She couldn't believe she'd never figured it out before. And now, Ginny felt like she might burst if she didn't tell someone *something*. The fact that Sportstatsguy and Mitch were the same person, the hacking, her crush on Mitch, and wishing he'd ask her to Homecoming. It was too much to keep secret.

"I have to tell you something," Ginny blurted, interrupting whatever Robin had been saying. She looked around and realized they were surrounded by people. Not wanting anyone to overhear, she grabbed Robin's elbow and lead her to the girls' locker room, which was always empty over lunch periods.

It had aisle upon aisle of red lockers to the left and bathrooms and showers to the right. Ginny walked to the last row, looking back and forth to confirm they were alone, and sat down on a wooden bench.

"This must be important!" Robin said, raising one eyebrow and taking a seat next to Ginny.

"Okay, you know Sportstatsguy? The guy I've been talking to online for more than a year?" Ginny started.

"He's coming to visit! He's coming to Homecoming with you! He's . . ." Robin started guessing, more excited with each one.

"He's Mitch Henry," Ginny admitted, watching for Robin's reaction.

Robin, who'd still been throwing out guesses, stopped mid-sentence, mouth open. "Wait, what?"

"Mitch is Sportstatsguy."

"Ginny!" Robin screeched. "Why didn't you tell me?!"

"I only found out like a month ago, and I have been trying to figure out how to tell *him* who *I* am."

"Wait, he doesn't know you are you?" Robin could barely contain herself.

"No, not yet," Ginny said quietly. She felt kind of bad about this but had never known how to bring it up.

Robin's eyes widened.

"I'm working on that, but I just couldn't keep it from you anymore," Ginny said.

"I'm going to need more information, young lady," Robin began, but was interrupted by the five-minute bell, which was particularly loud in the locker room.

Both girls jumped, then laughed at themselves and headed for the door.

"I'll tell you more later," Ginny promised. "Just don't tell anyone, obviously."

"Oh my gosh, Gin," Robin whispered as they entered the crowded hall. "We could double date! This is crazy!"

Robin squeezed her arm as they hurried to their locker. Ginny smiled and grabbed her phone and books. She was finally able to enjoy her crush with someone in real life.

6

MITCH

Mitch started mowing lawns for his parents the summer after he got hurt. He was stir crazy. After being on sports teams almost year round since he was little, being homeschooled and not being allowed to play football left him feeling antsy. Mom probably wouldn't have even let him do it if the riding lawn mower didn't give her motion sickness. But it did. She could barely make it through the front yard before she'd run inside for 7-Up and saltine crackers to soothe her upset stomach. Mitch saw it as an opportunity to do something outside. He was out mowing one day when old Mrs. Randall's daughter Sara waved him down.

"Hey, squirt," she said, ruffling his hair. The Randalls lived three doors down and Sara used to babysit him and Addie. Now she was married and had her own children. "So you're mowing lawns now, eh?"

Mitch hesitated. He didn't mow lawns plural. Just his own. "Yep," he said. "I started a lawn-mowing business."

Sara lifted an eyebrow and smiled. "I was hoping you'd say that. My dad isn't doing so great and I'm wondering what you'd charge to mow my parents' lawn once a week?"

"Fifteen dollars a week," he said before he even thought about it, or considered his mom's reaction when he had to tell her.

"You drive a tough bargain," she said. For a second, Mitch worried he'd asked for too much. "But I think I can handle that." Sara stuck her hand out and Mitch shook it. "It's a deal," she said. "Maybe when winter rolls around we can talk about shoveling?"

Mitch nodded, thinking of all the reasons his mom would think that was a terrible idea. "Yes! I shovel too!"

Sara smiled and waved before turning to walk back to her parents' house.

■ ■ ■

Mitch turned the engine on his mower and drove past the junior high and across the street. The wood rake and leaf blower that were mounted in a rack on the back rattled as he went over bumps in the road. His parents allowed him to have clients in a four-block radius of his house. He had as many clients as he could handle and was always being asked to take on more houses. The fact was, he charged less than "real" land-scaping companies and he was reliable. In the winter, he did the sidewalks for those same families, and he cleared drive-ways with his snowblower.

He turned down Virginia Avenue and looked ahead to the two houses he needed to get done before dinner. The Stegoras hired him after they had triplets a year ago. They were too busy dealing with babies to keep up with their landscaping. The other house was Ginny Ross's house. Ms. Ross saw him mowing next door one day, after Ginny's dad moved out, and asked if he could do their yard too. Mitch knew Professor Ross, and accepting the job felt almost like a betrayal. But he also felt like it was helping Ginny and her mom, which he was pretty sure Ginny's dad would want.

He opened the copper mailbox at the end of Ginny's long driveway and put in an envelope with "Mitch Henry Lawn Care" on the top left corner. He left bills in mailboxes every two weeks. It was more professional, and he got to avoid asking for money in person, which was always awkward. Mitch pulled large noise-canceling headphones from a compartment on the right side of his mower and placed them on his ears. He scrolled through the playlists on his phone, decided on a hip hop mix, and dropped the blades.

He never saw Ginny while he was working. He sometimes saw her around the neighborhood, but usually she was biking to or from school, or to Main Street. But he never saw her just hanging out at home. She always seemed like she was on some sort of mission, her wavy hair trailing behind as she pedaled past. Ginny was the kind of girl who had a million friends and was super involved with school. He was sure she was never bored or without things to do. Mitch wondered if he'd ever feel that way again. He shook his head as if to erase the thought, slowly making the wide turnaround to start the next line in the grass.

Mitch came to a stop next to the garage and cut the power. He took his headphones off and grabbed the leaf blower out of its mount. He'd been startled enough times by clients coming over to talk to him that he no longer listened to music when he wasn't actually mowing. He started blowing the leaves from the driveway and front walk when he saw motion out of the corner of his right eye. He turned off the blower and heard the tail end of a sentence.

"—ello, Mitch. How are you?" Ms. Ross walked over from where her SUV was parked in the driveway, her keys jangling in her hand.

"Good, thank you." Mitch stuck his hand out for Ms. Ross to shake. She seemed surprised but took it anyway. Her handshake wasn't firm like Sara's had been the day she got him started in this business. He'd shaken hands with clients ever since. It seemed like something a professional landscaper would do.

"Great. I'd like to schedule a leaf service with you, do you have your calendar?" She pulled her phone from the large purse slung over her arm.

Mitch pulled out and checked his phone. If he offered to do it this Saturday, he'd miss at least half of the college football games, but now that his podcast was at risk, he might need the money to save it. "I can do Saturday," he said, looking up. Ms. Ross was nodding and starting to type on her phone.

"Great," she pressed a button, looked up and smiled. "See you then, I've gotta grab my daughter." She turned and was soon backing out of the driveway.

She was all business. Mitch remembered how funny and nice Ginny's dad was and wondered how different it must be for Ginny to live only with her mom, who, if he was honest, seemed pretty cold.

Mitch finished entering the service into his phone calendar, which would also put it in his parents' calendar, and stuffed it in his back jeans pocket. This would get him an extra $30, and if he could convince the Stegoras to do their leaf service this weekend too, he'd be $60 richer. It wasn't much, but it was something. He wondered if there would be a way for him to take on more clients. His time was already pretty packed, but what else could he do?

He went back to blowing leaves from the walk of the Rosses' house. His mind drifted back to Ginny and what her life must be like without her dad. Maybe he'd been too presumptuous in thinking her life was perfect. At least his own parents, even at their busiest, were fun and affectionate.

Mitch returned the blower to its spot on the mower. Maybe he would ask Josh, or maybe even all of the guys, to do something outside of school. Instead of feeling sorry for himself, he should do something about it. It wasn't his old friends' fault for losing touch with Mitch, just like it wasn't his. He was old enough to take matters into his own hands.

Before he could lose his nerve he pulled his phone from his pocket and quickly typed out a text. He was as nervous as he would be if he was asking a girl out. Or inviting Rosco to meet in person.

Mitch Henry, 4:11pm: You guys want to come over Friday after school for pizza and then bike over to the football game?

Mitch stood looking at his phone and nothing happened. After a couple of minutes he returned the phone to his back pocket and started the mower. He needed to get the Stegoras' yard done and get home for dinner. He also had to ask his parents if his friends could come over for dinner on Friday. Maybe he'd wait until he knew if anyone even wanted to come over. As he drove next door, he felt a buzz under his butt. He stopped and checked his phone.

Josh Weinberg, 4:16pm: Mom says I can go. And to tell your mom hi.
Jin Zhao, 4:17pm: I'm in.
Zach Jameson, 4:18pm: Jin is always in if there's free food. LOL. I can go too.
Tyler Humphrey, 4:25pm: Yep.

Mitch read each response with increasing excitement. This was like having friends. *Actual* friends. Not the kind that you play video games with, or chat online with, that you've never met in person. He returned the phone to his pocket and dropped the blades of the mower. He hadn't felt this happy in a long time—not even close since he'd gotten the letter from Podder—and it felt good.

7

GINNY

Ginny slid into the blue chair in front of her computer at 8:30 p.m. After cheerleading practice, she and her mom went out for Chinese. They always went to dinner the Monday after her mom flew all weekend. Her mom would ask how Ginny's weekend was and then she would spend the rest of dinner telling her about the interesting people on the flight, or the famous people who had been particularly rude in first class, where she worked as lead flight attendant, or the handsome men her mom had met in the glamorous city she'd been to that weekend. Ginny loved hearing about the different places her mom traveled. She felt as though she'd been to many of the places herself simply by listening to all of her mom's stories of museums, cathedrals, and castle tours. But she hated the stories about her mom's dates in Paris or London or Rome. Ginny missed her dad.

"I got this from a street vendor in front of the Palais Garnier," her mom had said, using her best French accent and passing a thin box across the table. "Etienne and I had a few minutes to waste before the show, and I know you girls are wearing scarves a lot these days." Ginny opened the box and separated the peach tissue paper. She lifted the corners of the intricately folded material, and a large scarf with bright-colored swirls fell open. The tentative smile Ginny had when opening the box widened into a grin.

With a few swift arm movements, Ginny placed it perfectly around her neck, and she pulled her thick wavy hair from underneath the back. "I love it! How does it look?" She glanced up at her mom, who was aiming her phone at Ginny to take a picture.

"It's perfect! Now smile. I'm going to send a picture to Etienne. He helped me pick it out."

Ginny hesitated briefly, then focused her eyes at the phone and smiled.

Etienne was a former football player. Which really meant he was a former soccer player. Her mom told her that in most places outside the US, soccer was called football. She'd also told Ginny that Etienne was recognized nearly everywhere they went. She met him on a flight six months ago and now she saw him every chance she had when she flew to | Europe.

Mom spent the rest of dinner texting with Etienne. From time to time she'd relay what he was saying, but it was mostly like Ginny was there alone.

As Ginny powered up her laptop, she looked at the picture of her and her dad that sat on her desk in a bejeweled frame.

She sighed heavily. Her mom took the picture on one of their first visits to Chicago. Her dad had worked there for the past couple of years and she and her mom used to meet him on weekends if he couldn't come home to Minnesota. When they divorced a last year, the visits happened less and no longer involved Mom. She'd been hinting lately that he might visit sometime soon, but Ginny was starting to wonder if she was just saying it to make Ginny feel better.

Ginny heard the whine of her bedroom door opening and turned to find Lucky coming her way.

"Luckyloo," she said as she touched his nose with her own. "How's my boy?" Lucky answered by wagging his tail and Ginny rubbed behind his ears. "Such a good boy," she continued. She was tired, and had thirty-five pages to read for English, but she wanted to check in with Mitch.

Ginny was so relieved she'd finally told Robin about Mitch. It had been nearly impossible for Ginny to keep it from Robin, Emily, and Alicia. But she wasn't sure what she wanted to do just yet. They were her family in many ways and they usually told each other everything. When Ginny's parents first separated they said they wanted to keep Ginny's life "as normal as possible," which meant she would continue to live with her mom in their house, while her dad worked and lived in Chicago. Between missing her dad and knowing that her mom started dating after the divorce, Ginny felt like her heart might shatter into a million pieces. Her friends were there to offer comfort and to make her feel normal even though everything at home felt completely strange. Her friends, and Mitch too. They helped her stay positive and happy.

Looking back at the picture of her and her dad, Ginny felt a pang of guilt. He would not approve of her hacking. He might take interest in how she was doing it—he had once been a hacker himself, after all—but he most certainly wouldn't be pleased. While he'd spent his college years hacking, he was now the head of the Department of Information Management and Security at Chicago University.

Ginny's throat tightened. She didn't want to disappoint her dad. She squeezed her eyes shut to stop any ambitious tears and took a deep breath. Opening her eyes again, she returned her attention to her laptop and opened the Chatter icon at the lower righthand side of her screen.

Rosco: Hey you…

As she waited for Mitch to respond, she opened her English Lit book. She didn't want her eyes to wander or they'd fall on the picture of her dad again. Before she'd read a full paragraph she heard the chirp of an incoming message.

Sportstatsguy: Hey you - dinner with your mom tonight? Where was she this time?

Ginny's guilt and sadness about her parents slid away as she tapped her response.

Rosco: Paris. With Etienne. Again.
Sportstatsguy: Gross. Did she at least get you something good?
Rosco: Yes, a scarf! What'd you do tonight?

Sportstatsguy: Four lawns and Algebra. Lots of Algebra.
Rosco: Figure out what happened on your show last night?
Sportstatsguy: Nope, but people were bugging me about it all day.
Rosco: Oh no!
Sportstatsguy: It wasn't too bad. I might get more listeners?
Rosco: Are you still going to try to figure out who's doing it?
Sportstatsguy: I guess it depends on whether or not they do it
    again. Is that weird?
Rosco: No - I totally get it.

■ ■ ■

Ginny relaxed her shoulders and smiled. The next day, at school, Robin stood at their locker staring into the mirror as she separated the spiral curls on her head. Ginny was jealous of the way Robin could change her hair so drastically. Yesterday her hair was straight and long with the help of a weave. Today it stood on end, curls springing in every direction from her head.

"Yes!" Ginny said as she walked up behind Robin. "I love it!"

Robin looked sheepishly at Ginny. "My hair is kind of out of control. I hope Josh thinks it's cute." She turned back to the small mirror and picked at it carefully.

"It looks amazing and he will totally think so too," Ginny said as she unpacked her backpack.

Robin sighed and turned around, then pointed at Ginny's legs. "You look freezing!"

Ginny looked down at the red goose bumps across her skin. On game days cheerleaders wore their uniforms, and while they were allowed to wear leggings under their short pleated skirts, Ginny couldn't find a clean pair in her drawers or even a dirty pair in the hamper.

"Yeah. I am cold." She peered into their small mirror and tugged at the top of the ponytail she'd put in when she left home. "Come on. Let's go, Curly." She grabbed her books and slammed the locker door, causing the chandelier to fall, again.

Robin shook her free fist at the ceiling in exasperation. "Ginny!" She started laughing and shook her head as they started walking to Advisory.

They turned the corner and Ginny automatically narrowed her eyes and looked down the hall to the left. She could see Mitch's tall form, but today it was just him and Josh. He grabbed his books, shut his locker, and they walked away. Ginny shook her head in disappointment and kept walking, trying to tune into what Robin was saying.

" . . . cheering the JV football game tonight, aren't you? You'll be home in time to hear Mitch's show, right? I wonder if he'll do another *The Whole Truth* thing. It's so weird."

Ginny's mind was racing. "Yeah, JV football. I'm not sure I'll be home in time." Robin stopped to say hi to Josh, but Ginny walked straight into Advisory. She slid into her seat, the bare skin of her thighs making a screeching noise on the metal. She had to think of what to do next on Mitch's show. Reality Radio was going to have to get a little juicier to get the attention and listeners that Mitch needed.

■ ■ ■

Ginny faced the bleachers from the sidelines of the football field. They were filling up quickly. She looked back and forth, trying to find a place to put her phone so it could record the squad's cheers. "Any ideas?" she asked Robin, who stood on the other side of the chain-link fence that surrounded the field. Robin walked over to a white plastic sign that read "HOME" and reached behind it.

"This might work," Robin said as she wiggled it gently. Ginny walked over and wedged her phone between it and the fence. She kicked the metal a few times to be sure the phone was secure, then adjusted it so the camera had an unobstructed view of the cheerleaders that stood behind her.

"Perfect," Ginny said as she pressed the red record button.

"You're welcome," Robin said. She waved a gloved hand and then climbed the bleachers to sit with Alicia and Emily.

Ginny rejoined the line of seven cheerleaders and bent to grab her pompoms. "Okay, get ready, the song will start any minute." The girls straightened in their line and stood with their hands at their hips looking expectantly at the growing crowd.

The PA crackled and a tinny voice echoed across the field. "Kenwood Fans! Are you ready to watch some football?" The crowd stood and clapped. As the school song began to play from the speakers, Ginny stepped forward and clapped her pompoms together once, a sign to the rest of the girls that they were about to get started. Their sharp movements were precise as they cheered and danced through the song. They then marched and clapped into a different formation and two of the smaller girls were thrust high into the air. The girls who remained on the ground moved quickly to catch them and they all finished the song by falling gracefully into splits. Ginny looked at the girls on either side of her, their breaths producing white bursts of cold air, and grinned. They'd done this at the beginning of every game they'd cheered this year, but it was the first time they'd done it without any mistakes. When she looked up at the crowd she saw Robin cupping her hands around her mouth and yelling "woo-hoo!" and Emily giving her two thumbs up.

At half-time Ginny led the squad in an intricate cheer that had two of the girls standing on others' shoulders, falling straight back, and then being lifted up again. Ginny had found it on YouTube one Sunday morning at Book Nook. It was the first time they'd tried the cheer in public and she couldn't wait to get home to watch the video her phone was recording.

The second half of the game seemed to last forever. Her friends left after her half-time cheer, too cold to remain in the stands. Mitch's podcast would be on in a few hours, and Ginny didn't have a new segment. She needed to get home to figure something out.

After winning 27-7, the football players ran off the field through the two lines the cheerleaders had formed. She clapped and saw Josh running at the back of the team.

"Hey, Ginny," he said, holding his helmet up in a sort of wave.

"Good game," she said, raising a pompom.

As she walked back to the school with the other girls, Ginny texted her mom to tell her she was ready to be picked up. Once inside the front doors of the junior high, she sat on a marble bench, glad to be out of the cold. She pulled out her phone and saw that it was almost dead. She opened the video and pushed play. She'd been right, the school song routine was perfect. She fast forwarded to find the half-time cheer, then found that she'd gone too far. She pulled back and pressed play. She watched herself and the other cheerleaders yelling and clapping. She pulled forward again, trying to stop at the right time to catch the cheer before the phone died. When she pushed play she realized she still hadn't gone far enough. She was about to pull forward again when she heard talking over the noise of the crowd.

" . . . ssshhhhh. Robin is here!"

"Sorry, Becca. But what is the plan?"

"I'm going to ask to be excused from gym . . ."

Ginny gripped the phone and stared open-mouthed as a red battery graphic blinked three times before the screen turned black.

8

MITCH

"Stop it! You're shaking the whole table!" Addie swatted Mitch's thigh. He tugged lightly on her ponytail in response. He couldn't sit still.

"Why so antsy?" Dad asked from the stove, where he was scooping beef stroganoff and noodles onto the empty plate Mitch's mom was holding in front of him.

"Do we have anything going on Friday?" Mitch asked.

"I think we actually have an entire weekend with no activities, except for volunteering Saturday night," Mom said, setting the plate in front of Addie. "Why? What's up?"

"Can Josh, Tyler, Jin, and Zach come over for pizza? Then we'll bike over to the football game at the high school. Is that okay?"

Mom's eyebrows shot up.

"Of course! Great idea!" Dad sat down and held up his fist from across the kitchen table for Mitch to bump with his own.

"Can I have friends over too?" Addie asked, mouth full of food.

Mitch looked at her sideways. Addie had sleepovers and play dates with friends all the time. Other than Rosco, and the people Mitch played on his Xbox who lived a million miles away, he hadn't had friends since his mom pulled him out of school. The least Addie could do was let him have one night without her and her friends pestering him.

"No, you don't need to have people over. Maybe you could go to someone else's house, but Mitch and his friends will be plenty." Mitch looked at his mom, who was sitting back in her chair and smiling. She looked relieved. He knew his parents worried about him.

"But Moooooommmm . . ."

"Adelaide? No." Mitch was pretty sure his mom could silence world leaders with one of her looks. Addie went back to eating her dinner without another word.

Mitch stuffed a forkful of beef stroganoff into his mouth and tried to keep from grinning.

The person Mitch really wanted to talk to was Rosco. He knew his parents understood how huge this was, but they were his *parents*. Rosco was the only one who would really get it. She knew what it was like to be lonely. For her it wasn't a lack of friends, it was the lack of a family. Her mom traveled all the time, and even when she was home, she wasn't really *there*. Her dad had moved away, and Rosco missed him like crazy.

■ ■ ■

Mitch flipped the sign that hung on his bedroom door so the "ON AIR" side faced out and then shut the door. Addie had burst in asking him to play Barbies while he was recording his podcast too many times. He finally made the sign, which *usually* stopped her from making another embarrassing cameo on his sports show.

He put his headphones on and opened Podder. He watched the clock on the top right of his screen, and when it hit 7 p.m. he pushed play on the school song. When he was little and his parents put him and Addie to bed, they used to sing the University of MN rouser song before they kissed them goodnight and turned the lights out. It was the first song he'd ever learned the words to. He loved playing it at the beginning of his show. He took a deep breath and pulled his head from one shoulder to the other. He did this before every show even though talking into a microphone didn't *actually* require stretching. It was a holdover habit from football.

"Welcome to the Tuesday edition of *Sports with Mitch*. For those of you who are new to this podcast, thanks for listening! I'm hoping some of you will call in tonight to tell me all about the Kenwood Junior High football game. I heard about the high school soccer game, and apparently it was painful. For the Brookhood Cougars that is."

Mitch chuckled silently at his own joke. He'd thought it up while studying Spanish vocabulary words after dinner.

"We also have to talk Monday Night Football. Let's start with . . ." and then all he heard in his headphones was static. It was happening, *again*. In all of the excitement over his friends coming over on Friday, Mitch had nearly forgotten that his show might get hacked.

He took several breaths. He wasn't going to freak out like he did the first time this happened. This time he knew that no matter what he did, he wouldn't be able to stop it; someone far smarter than him was hacking him. His computer programming skills were no match for whoever was doing this. He sat back in his chair and closed his eyes.

"Welcome to *The Whole Truth*. Tonight we have a confession," said an electronic-sounding girl's voice.

"Ssshhhhh. Robin is here!"

"Sorry, Becca. But what is the plan?"

Mitch sat up and opened his eyes wide. Wait. Becca?! This had something to do with Becca? And Robin?

"I'm going to ask to be excused from gym. I'll say I don't feel well or something. And I'm going to take her phone from her locker and text Josh something that looks like it was meant for someone else."

"Like what?"

"I don't know, something like," Becca paused and the sound of the crowd cheering replaced her voice. "Did he just get a touchdown? He did. YEAH, JOSH!"

Mitch shook his head. He couldn't believe this was about people he knew. He couldn't even imagine what school would be like tomorrow. Or how many calls he'd get after this was over.

"Anyway, something like "I don't want to go to Homecoming with him. I never should have said yes, I don't even like him." He will think Robin is talking about him to her friends and he will freak out." Becca almost sounded bored as she rattled off her plan.

Mitch recoiled and backed up from his desk. This wasn't cool, this was personal. Becca was coming after his friends and some mystery person was using *him* to expose her. He felt a little sick. It was like he and his friends were puppets in someone else's game.

"Do you think he will dump her as his Homecoming date?" Lily asked, still talking quietly, probably for fear of Becca's wrath.

Becca cackled. "Umm . . . yeah. And then who will he run to?" The crowd cheered and the sound transitioned to static. Then silence.

Mitch was mad, but it was mostly on behalf of his friends. At the sound of silence, he looked up at his screen. It appeared that he had control again and he pulled the microphone close to his lips.

"Well, I guess that evil plan has been thwarted!" He chuckled nervously and then, without missing a beat, went back to talking about the soccer game as if nothing happened. It was the only way he could think of to beat the hacker. As his mom always advised when discussing unkind or drama-prone friends and classmates, "ignore, ignore, ignore."

9

GINNY

"Ginny! You need to walk this dog!" Mom yelled from downstairs.

Ginny looked at the clock on her nightstand. She could not, under any circumstances, leave now. Mitch's podcast was just about to end. She wanted to hear how he closed the show. She wanted to see what would happen on KenChat when it was over. She needed proof that all of this was actually worth it. Would he get the listeners he needed to keep his show? That just had to happen!

"GENEVIEVE! NOW!" Ginny got up from her desk. When Mom used her full name she meant business. This could not be happening. There wasn't a short enough walk route to get back before his podcast ended. She'd miss Mitch's reaction and what callers might say. She kicked off her slippers and stuffed her feet into the Nike running shoes that were under her bed. She tied her shoes, grabbed her cheerleading jacket to throw over her sweatshirt and leggings, and stomped down the stairs. Hoping to make her unhappiness known. Mom walked right past her, up the stairs, without acknowledging the injustice she was inflicting. She was actually *smirking*.

Lucky was at the bottom of the stairs with the red rubber donut that squeaked in his mouth. He jumped around in circles, like a bucking bronco, squeaking over and over. Despite Ginny's annoyance, she couldn't help but smile. Poor Lucky got way fewer walks since Dad left. She didn't think he needed a walk right this second, however.

"Lucky, you are *sassy* tonight!" Ginny rubbed his head as she walked toward the mud room. He dropped his toy and followed her enthusiastically. She rummaged through the bin labeled "LUCKY," sighing heavily. She couldn't believe she was going to miss the rest of Mitch's show. She found a flashlight that worked, but Lucky's retractable leash was nowhere to be found. She opened the other bins, finding hats, mittens, even poop-scoop bags, but no leash.

"Looking for this?" Ginny's eyes got wide and she spun around. The leash hung from Dad's pointer finger, and he grinned. She almost knocked him over as she lunged for him.

"Dad," she screamed into his shoulder. He smelled the same as he always did. A combination of shaving cream and minty cologne. His cheek was rough—he hadn't shaved today.

"Rosco, my love! How 'bout we walk our Lucky?" He stepped back and looked at her. "I'm not sure I approve of this," he said as he put his hand on top of Ginny's head and brought it to his chest, measuring her height. She had grown half an inch since he was last home.

"What are you doing here?" Ginny couldn't believe he was standing in front of her. She hadn't seen him in more than a month.

Her mom was coming down the stairs with the larger of her two travel bags and wearing her navy-and-red flight attendant uniform. "I'm on call this week and found out this morning that I needed to be on a flight to Turkey. I'll be gone through Monday, and Grandma is in Arizona. I told you that Dad and I have been talking about him coming for a weekend. It just happened to work for him to come today." Dad met her halfway down the stairs and took her suitcase from her. He opened the front door, where Ginny could see a yellow cab waiting in the street. They may be divorced, but some things will never change. Dad wasn't the kind of guy to watch someone else carry something even remotely heavy.

"You'll be okay?" Mom pulled Ginny into a hug and kissed her on top of her head. Ginny was speechless. *Okay*?! She'd be more than okay. She'd be *great*. "Ginny?" Mom held her at arm's length and looked at her, worried.

"Yes! We'll be okay!" Ginny felt like she might explode.

Mom let go and grabbed her purse off the hall table. "Okay, I will check in with you guys tomorrow. Love you." she blew Ginny another kiss and smiled and nodded at Dad.

As soon as the front door shut Dad said, "Okay, Luckyloo, car ride?" He took the car keys from the hook that hung inside the door that led to the garage. Lucky bounced after him.

"Ice cream?" Ginny asked, hopefully.

"You betcha!" he yelled over his shoulder "YES!!!"

■ ■ ■

Ginny, her dad, and Lucky were the only customers in The Drip, and Ms. Kelly was sweeping the floor around them.

"Rachel, there is no place in the world that has better coffee chip ice cream. You need to put this in cartons and sell it!"

Ms. Kelly shook her head and rolled her eyes, laughing. Ginny giggled. Her dad knew what to say to make anyone feel good. Mitch was like that too. He actually reminded her a lot of her dad.

"Did you finish your project, Ginny?" Ms. Kelly asked as she flipped the chairs to hang upside down on the newly cleaned tables.

Ginny's brow furrowed as she ate another spoonful.

"The one you were working on last weekend?"

Ginny nearly spit out her ice cream. "Oh, yes," she croaked before coughing. Dad patted her back as she tried to clear what had gone down the wrong tube.

Lucky jumped up from under the table and barked at the commotion, tail wagging.

"We'll get out of your hair so you can close up," Dad said, tossing his empty cup into the garbage and reattaching Lucky's leash to his collar.

"It was good to see you," Ms. Kelly said as she bent to look Lucky in the eyes and he licked her chin. "I only get to see Ginny these days!" She stood up and smiled at Dad.

"Good to see you too, Rachel, give my best to Julie." Dad took Ginny's empty cup and threw hers away too.

"I will, she'll be sorry she missed you!" Julie was Rachel's wife but she hadn't been at The Drip very much since they'd adopted baby Aamiina from Somalia. Ms. Kelly followed them to the door, the bell jingling as they opened it, and locked it behind them.

Ginny missed this. Feeling like she was part of the community. She still saw all of these people, but when she was alone it seemed like they looked at her like she was an orphan. Dad knew everyone, talked to everyone, and knew about their lives. Mom wasn't nearly as comfortable talking to people. She smiled a lot, and made small talk, but she never seemed to warm up to people. Not like Dad.

He turned toward Book Nook and then looked at his watch. "Holy Hannah! We need to get you home to bed! You have school tomorrow." He put his arm around her neck, an affectionate headlock, and they walked toward Mom's SUV. Ginny thought it was kind of funny that Dad was driving Mom's car—with the license plate that said LISBETH. Mom got personalized plates when she got the new car after the divorce.

Ginny climbed in, displacing Lucky, who had jumped into her seat from Dad's side. Dad found a station playing a rap song that had to be at least twenty years old. He turned the volume up and danced in his seat as he pulled out of the parking spot. Ginny leaned her head back and closed her eyes. Her cheeks hurt from smiling, and Dad had only been home for an hour. For the first time in ages, Ginny felt like she could relax. Like someone else was taking care of her instead of her having to take care of herself.

■ ■ ■

Ginny had forgotten her phone at home, and she barely thought about Mitch or the hack, or anything, frankly, since the moment she saw her dad. When she got back to her computer, she saw a message waiting for her in Chatter and opened the window.

Sportstatsguy: You'll never guess what happened!

Ginny smiled nervously. She knew what happened during the show, but she wasn't sure if anything had happened after it ended. She was eating ice cream with her dad, which she still couldn't believe.

Rosco: Were you hacked again???
Sportstatsguy: No. I mean, yes, but that's not what I'm talking about.

Ginny cocked her head to the side. She thought he'd be excited, or at least would want to talk about tonight's hack. It involved people he knew, for crying out loud!

Rosco: What happened?

She stared at the screen nervously, waiting for Mitch's response. It took a while but finally he wrote back.

> *Sportstatsguy: Sorry, mom is yelling at me to go to bed. But I invited the guys, my old friends, over on Friday for pizza and then to the football game. And all of them are coming!*
> *Rosco: That is amazing! You'll never guess what happened to me!*
> *Sportstatsguy: You opened a new zone on the map in Final Fantasy 15?*
> *Rosco: That too, but no. My dad is here!!! Until Monday!!!*
> *Sportstatsguy: Shut up! So both of us had like the best night ever?*
> *Rosco: Apparently!*

Ginny smiled at the screen. She had her dad and she kind of had Mitch. Her heart felt like it might burst.

> *Sportstatsguy: Okay, now Mom is threatening my life. Talk tomorrow? I want to hear about your dad!*
> *Rosco: Tomorrow. Can't wait to hear about your friends!*
> Ginny remembered the hack.
> *Rosco: And what happened tonight on your podcast!*

Curious, Ginny opened KenChat. It was blowing up! More of Ginny's friends were posting because this time they actually knew who was involved. New posts were going up so fast it was hard to keep up with what people were saying. As Ginny started to read, her phone buzzed. When she tore her eyes from KenChat she saw that it was Robin calling. She'd gotten so wrapped up in Mitch, and other people's reactions, that she hadn't thought to call Robin herself. Her face flushed with embarrassment as she answered the phone.

"Ginny, did you hear that?" Robin's voice was quiet and urgent.

Ginny looked down, ashamed. "I was just about to call you," she lied.

"Why would Becca do that? I'm so embarrassed."

"I don't know, Robs. Have you talked to Josh?"

"He didn't hear it. He's out to dinner with his family. I told him to call me later."

"Are you okay?" Ginny's chest was tightening. Maybe she hadn't thought this through. If her dad knew what she was doing he would be so disappointed in her.

"I don't know. I'm humiliated."

"I'm sure anyone who heard it knows this isn't about you. It's all Becca."

"I just hope tomorrow doesn't suck."

Ginny was trying to focus on what Robin was saying, but it was getting harder and harder to ignore KenChat. When she glanced up at her screen she saw that many more comments had gone up since Robin called. She wondered what Becca would do. She made a mental note to check Becca's page when she was done talking to Robin.

"Do you want to come over after school tomorrow? Maybe go shopping?" Ginny asked.

Robin cheered a little at this. "I need to find a dress for Homecoming. Could we do that?"

"Sure! And don't worry, I think school will be fine."

"I hope you're right," Robin took a deep breath. "See you tomorrow."

"See you tomorrow." Ginny tapped the red "end" button on her phone and sighed. She didn't want Robin to be sad or embarrassed, but she was sure nobody would think poorly of Robin. Becca, on the other hand. She looked up at the screen and saw that many more comments had been posted. People were so excited that they knew who the secret was about. Even without names, the voices (and attitudes) were recognizable.

Ginny remembered to check Becca's page. She searched her name and was shocked at the messages people had left her.

What is wrong with you?

You are so mean!

How could you do this to Robin? She would never be this cruel.

Jealous much???

You're horrible.

You're pathetic.

You're disgusting.

Ginny stared, mouth agape. She'd thought a variation of all of those things, but she would never have actually said any of it to Becca, or posted it. She couldn't believe people were so mean. Becca herself hadn't posted anything since she'd been at the football game earlier that evening. Typically, she posted pictures and snide comments, but tonight she was unusually quiet. Ginny almost felt sorry for her. It wouldn't be easy to have people attacking something you'd never meant to be public. Even if it was an evil plan that you were about to carry out.

"I'm doing this for Mitch," she whispered. "For Mitch," she repeated.

There was a soft knock on Ginny's bedroom door, and she turned to see Lucky jumping up on her bed and Dad peeking in.

"Rosco, my love, time for bed." He nudged Lucky to get down and started moving Ginny's stuffed animals, making room for her to climb under the covers. She closed her laptop, thinking "for Mitch" one last time, and turned off her desk lamp.

When Ginny was snug in bed, Dad leaned down and kissed her. "You're my smart and beautiful girl, and I love you very much." Her throat tightened. She didn't know why hearing that made her feel like crying, but it did. Dad hadn't been home at bedtime in ages, but he used to say this to her every single night.

"Love you too, Daddy," Ginny said in a quiet voice. He flipped the light switch and shut the door behind him. She could hear him singing as he walked down the hall and then downstairs. She shut her eyes feeling happier, safer, and more like a kid than she had in what seemed like forever.

10

MITCH

Mitch cleaned and assembled his saxophone as his classmates streamed into the band room. When he was homeschooled he took private lessons at a local music shop owned by Bobby B. Vance. Bobby was at least seventy years old, with a goatee and a beret. Mitch thought he was probably once a great jazz player in New York or Chicago who had retired in the suburbs of Minneapolis. Bobby held recitals with all of his students, but they performed pieces by themselves. Now that he was back at school, Mitch still wasn't quite used to playing with a group, but after last week's concert he felt better about his place in it.

"Okay, everyone, let's go to page twenty-four in your *Essential Elements* book." Today his new band teacher, Mr. Swan, was wearing caramel-colored boots, blue jeans, a red flannel shirt, and suspenders. He looked like a stylish lumberjack. Mitch smiled as he turned the pages in his band book. He loved Mr. Swan. He thought this was probably what Bobby B. Vance was like when he was younger.

They were working on songs that Mitch already knew. He played along, but his mind wandered. It wasn't even lunchtime yet, and the day had already been weird. When he got to school there were people waiting for him at his locker. They wanted to talk about what they heard Becca say the night before. Nobody had seen her yet, and Lily was supposed to be in this class. She played clarinet, but she wasn't here.

"Okay, how about we go to page—" Mr. Swan started. "Well, Ms. Franken! Good of you to join us!" Mitch looked up and saw Lily making her way to her chair. "Page fifty, please," Mr. Swan finished.

When she got to her seat, Lily looked over at Mitch and gave him the angriest look he'd ever seen her give. He returned his attention to his music book and turned the pages quickly. He could feel Lily staring.

Mitch spent the rest of class looking either at his music or straight ahead at Mr. Swan. He didn't dare look even slightly left, where he might catch a glimpse of Lily. When the bell rang Mitch took his time disassembling his sax. He saw Lily rush out and breathed a sigh of relief. After securing the brass locks on his sax case he headed for the door.

Wednesday was chicken strips day, and for some reason the junior high had the best chicken strips Mitch had ever tasted. Usually on Wednesdays, he ran to the cafeteria, but today he took his time. He found Josh at the end of the lunch line.

"Have you seen Becca yet?" Josh asked, talking quieter than usual. Mitch looked around, expecting to see her coming his way.

"No, why, have you?" Mitch nudged Josh to move up in line.

"Robin said she saw her come into school late." Josh gave his lunch account number to the woman at the cash register and grabbed a chocolate milk.

"How is," Mitch started and then faced the cashier, "47732. Thanks!" He took a skim milk and followed Josh to a lunch table by the windows.

"How is Robin?" Mitch said as they sat down next to Taylor, Zach, and Jin, and he saw Emily and Alicia on the other side of them. Robin and Ginny were still in line for lunch.

"Okay. Mostly just embarrassed."

Mitch inhaled two of his six chicken strips, smothered in barbecue sauce, while Tyler and Jin talked about an upcoming science project. He looked around and felt, for the first time this school year, like he actually belonged here. He started to dip another strip in sauce when suddenly the cafeteria got eerily quiet. He looked up to see Becca storming towards his table.

"This is *your* fault! You did this!" Becca practically spit her words at Mitch.

He set his chicken down and said, "Becca, I swear, I have no idea who is hacking my podcast." He actually felt bad. He really didn't know who was doing this, or why.

Becca's eyes were puffy and red and it looked like she came to school in her pajamas. "Right. Just because you don't have friends, that's not my problem. Stop using other people to get them!"

Mitch felt slapped. By now, a small crowd had gathered around the table.

"Becca, stop it," Josh said, standing up to face her.

"Stay out of it!" she hissed.

Mitch had never seen Becca so mad. She was generally disagreeable but never this out of control.

Mitch saw Robin set down her tray and turn toward Becca. "If this is anyone's fault, it's yours," she said. "You were the one planning to lie about me. You're the one who got caught. Don't take it out on other people." Robin was shaking, she was so angry. Everyone was still, waiting to see what Becca would say next.

Becca's angry face fell a little and Mitch thought she might start crying. A lump formed in his throat as he saw through her mean exterior, even if just for a second. Then she looked angry again.

"Whatever!" Becca pushed her way back through the crowd and walked directly into Ginny, sending her lunch tray flying and Ginny falling to the ground. "Sorry," Becca said quietly, stifling a sob. As Ginny's tray and food clattered to the ground around her, Becca ran from the cafeteria, her hands covering her face.

Mitch jumped up and offered Ginny a hand to help her up.

"Sorry," he started. "I didn't realize . . ." he trailed off, not knowing what to say.

"It's okay, not your fault," Ginny said, brushing crispy chicken crumbs from her front. "I guess I need a new lunch," she said, laughing a little awkwardly.

Mitch sat down again and looked at his food. He'd lost his appetite. He could hear people congratulating Robin for standing up to Becca, but he couldn't participate.

"Hey, are you going to eat that?" Jin asked, pointing to Mitch's chicken. Mitch shook his head and Jin took the paper bowl.

"I feel bad," he said, too quiet for anyone to hear.

"Huh?" Jin asked.

"It's my fault," he said, finally looking up at his friends. "I mean, I'm not doing it, but it's on *my* podcast. I kind of feel responsible."

"No offense, dude, but I don't think anyone here thinks you're smart enough to do something like this," Zach said, grinning. This even made Mitch laugh.

"Seriously, though," Josh started before guzzling his entire chocolate milk. He let out a loud "aaahhhhhh" after slamming down the empty carton. "Nobody thinks you're doing this on purpose. Don't worry about it. Becca will get over it."

Mitch wasn't actually sure if she would.

■ ■ ■

When the last bell rang, Mitch ran to his locker to pack up his stuff. He had two lawns to mow and a lot of reading to do, but tonight he had another mission. He was going to take care of whoever was messing with his podcast. He'd come up with a brilliant plan but he couldn't do it alone. He only knew one person who could help. Rosco's time would be more limited than usual with her dad's visit, but he knew she'd want to help if she could. He ran the lengths of the athletic fields to his house and went straight to his room.

"Hello to you too," Mom called after him. He sat down in front of his laptop and started typing.

Sportstatsguy: Hey you!

Mitch sat watching the black Chatter window. "Come on! Please be online!" He got up and pulled sweats out of his bottom drawer to change into for mowing. He grabbed a well-worn baseball cap off of a rack that hung on his closet door and heard a chirp from his computer.

> *Rosco: Hey you!*
> *Sportstatsguy: I have to go mow a couple of lawns, and I know you're probably busy with your dad, but can you maybe help me later? I have an idea to save my podcast but will need your tech genius.*

He hoped that made her smile. It was true. She was so good at programming and coding. She was even ridiculously good at gaming. Sometimes she streamed herself playing games to help other gamers figure out how to make it to higher levels.

> *Rosco: Well...if it's a genius you need...I GUESS I could make time. Ha! How about 8?*
> *Sportstatsguy: Perfect! It's a date.*

He pushed send before he realized what he'd just said. A date?! It's not really what he meant . . . but . . . it wasn't like he didn't *like* her. He did. His thoughts were interrupted by a chirp.

> *Rosco: Talk to you at 8 - don't be late!*

Mitch laughed, nervously. He looked at the time and realized he had to get going if he was going to be able to be back at his desk by then.

> *Sportstatsguy: Okay, later!*
> *Rosco: Later!*

11

GINNY

"I can't believe Becca went off on Mitch like that," Ginny said, each step making loud rustling noises as she kicked through the piles of leaves gathered at the side of the road.

"I know, but I'm almost glad she did because I got to tell her off too. And that girl deserved it!" Robin blew into her hands and rubbed them together. It was chilly and neither of them had gloves.

That morning Ginny asked her dad to take her and Robin to the mall after school and then dinner. Robin needed to start looking for a Homecoming dress, and Ginny wanted to look too. Just in case she got to go. "So where do you want to look for dresses?"

Robin kicked leaves in Ginny's direction and wiggled her eyebrows up and down. "I saw some pretty ones in the widow of Juju's, so I want to start there. What about you?"

Ginny kicked leaves back. "I will look but I don't have a date like you do."

"Well, you might have a date if you tell a certain someone who you really are," Robin said as they turned into Ginny's driveway.

They could hear music playing from Ginny's house before they even got to the front door.

Robin hooked her arm through Ginny's for the last few steps. "Awww, I've missed your dad!"

They walked in and it was like Ginny was transported to a time before her parents were divorced. Michael Jackson was playing and they could hear her dad singing from the kitchen. The microwave beeped its conclusion and whatever was in there smelled good.

Dad was pulling a full plate of nachos out of the microwave and Lucky was jumping around and his nose was in the air, sniffing. "Girls! We'll head to the mall shortly. Tell me what we're shopping for over nachos!" He set the plate down on the kitchen island and pulled out three smaller plates from the cupboard and a jar of salsa from the fridge.

"*Robin* is looking for a Homecoming dress!" Ginny said, scooping salsa onto a large cheese-covered chip.

"Reeaaalllyyy. And who, may I ask, are you going to Homecoming with?"

"Josh Weinberg," Robin said as she stuffed two large chips into her mouth.

"He was in my kindergarten and first grade classes, do you remember him?" Ginny asked.

Dad nodded as he finished chewing. "His dad, Ari, is my chiropractor. In fact, I should try to get in to see him while I'm home. Okay, so Homecoming dress for Robin. What are you looking for, Rosco?"

"Nothing really, just shopping with Robs."

"She's looking for a Homecoming *date* at the mall," Robin joked. Ginny elbowed her.

"Well, I hear junior high boyfriends are on sale at Macy's," Dad winked and took one last chip with salsa. "We should probably get a move on before all the good ones are gone!"

Robin guffawed and Ginny said, "Hardy har har. Let me run upstairs for my bag."

■ ■ ■

They walked into Kendale Mall and first stopped at the cafe inside of Macy's. Dad set his backpack down on one of the tables and made the girls sit there until he came back with coffee.

"I'll be here working. Let me know if you need anything, or if you find something really great that you don't have the money for, okay? Otherwise I need you back here by 6 p.m. and then we'll grab dinner before heading home." He pulled a small silver laptop out of his bag and opened it up. Because he worked in computers, he'd always been able to work almost anywhere. As long as he could set up his laptop, he was able to get stuff done. But now, with his college job, he had to work on-site in Chicago. Ginny and Robin started walking away and he called after them. "Hey! I expect you to be respectful, okay?" They nodded and turned down the aisle that would bring them out into the mall.

Juju's was a large boutique that sold clothes for teens and young adults. They had a big dress section that was always elaborately decorated for the season. When they walked through the front door, they could see bright-colored leaves hanging from the ceiling in the back right corner.

"Welcome to Juju's, are you looking for anything special?" A girl with long brown curly hair, a gold nose ring, and a name tag that said "Andi" stood at a table full of jeans, refolding them so the labels on the front zipper faced out.

"Homecoming dresses," Robin said, smiling shyly.

"Fun!" said Andi. She dropped the jeans she'd been folding and said, "Follow me!"

Ginny and Robin could have easily found them on their own, but she seemed happy to have the diversion.

"Dresses on this side are probably for older girls, like high school and college, but this side has tons of options you'll love," Andi waved her arms like Ginny's mom did when she was pointing out exit rows on an airplane.

Ginny felt a pang of guilt. She hadn't thought of her mom once since her dad showed up. This is the kind of thing she would have loved to do with Ginny. It's just that this isn't what Ginny loved to do most of the time. She liked to shop with her friends, but shopping with her mom always felt like work.

"Ooohhh, look at this!" Robin held up a plum-colored taffeta dress.

Ginny nodded and smiled as she started looking. There were so many styles and colors. She wanted so badly to be shopping for herself. Her eyes settled on a sleeveless fit-and-flare emerald-green satin one.

"Robin, you have to try this one. This color would look so good on you!" She handed it to Robin, who was holding three others.

"Gin, you need to try things on too. I *know* someone is going to ask you and you need to be prepared."

Ginny started gathering dresses to try on. When both of their arms were too full to hold more, they went to the back of the store to start trying them on. She was trying to zip up the back when she heard Robin say something, her voice muffled by the floor-to-ceiling walls. Ginny cracked her door open. "Did you say something?"

Robin came out in a really low-cut light-blue satin gown that made her look twenty-five years old instead of thirteen.

Ginny made a face.

"That bad, huh?" Robin looked in the three-way mirror in the large common area of the dressing room. "Yikes."

"It might be really cute, in like, ten years." Ginny came all the way out of her room, holding the taffeta material up under the arms.

"Turn around." Robin zipped up the back and clasped the hook at the top.

Ginny turned around and looked in the mirror, standing on her tiptoes to get the full affect. The navy dress had a V-neck and a thin belt at the waist, and then it puffed out. It even had pockets!

"Oh my gosh, Gin," Robin put her hand to her mouth.

"How's everything going in—oh, wow. That looks amazing on you! Your date won't know what hit him!" Andi emptied the other rooms and walked back into the store with her arms full.

Ginny looked at herself in the mirror and wondered what it would be like standing next to Mitch. She'd never felt so pretty.

"Can you take a picture? I should probably send it to my mom." Ginny pulled her phone from her bag and handed it to Robin. She put her hands on her hips, feeling awkward, and Robin took a picture.

"I'm going to try on the green one you found. You don't need to try on any of the others, you've already found 'the one.'" Robin turned for Ginny to unzip her and then slipped back into her room.

"Wait, did you say something before?" Ginny asked, loudly enough for Robin to hear through the door.

"Oh, yeah, when are you going to tell Mitch?"

Ginny froze. It was the question she hadn't allowed herself to really consider. She could hear the rustling of taffeta coming from the other side of the door.

"Gin? Did you hear me?" Robin came out and twirled.

"Robs! You look so pretty!" Ginny looked in the mirror with her. The deep emerald green glowed against Robin's dark skin. And it looked great with the navy Ginny was wearing.

"It's like we're about to walk the red carpet or something," Robin said, putting her arm around Ginny's shoulders. "We should be models. Seriously."

They both laughed, striking poses. "You guys look great! Do you want me to take your picture?" Andi asked as she took Ginny's phone. "Okay, say, 'We're the prettiest girls at Homecoming!'"

"We're the prettiest girls at Homecoming," Ginny and Robin said, trying to hold their smiles, arms around each other.

"Well, Gin, I think we're done here!" Robin turned around so Ginny could unzip her, then Ginny did the same. Then they both went back into their rooms to change back into normal clothes.

After Robin paid for her dress and Ginny put hers on hold, they walked back into the mall.

"Should we look for shoes?" Ginny asked, looking in both directions.

Robin pointed left and they walked back toward Macy's. "So you never answered me. When are you going to tell Mitch?"

Ginny couldn't delay anymore. "Oh, right. I guess I don't know. Why?"

"First, how did this happen?" Robin said. "When did you know Sportstatsguy was Mitch?"

Ginny took a deep breath. She'd been wanting to share this with Robin and her other friends for months but hadn't felt ready until now. "So remember? He got hit by that car in sixth grade? He broke both legs and his pelvis, and it took a really long time for him to recover. He had to heal, and then do a ton of physical therapy to even be able to walk normal again, and he was really weak." They turned into Macy's and veered left to the shoe department.

"Right! And it's not like any of us had phones back then. So Josh didn't really keep in touch with him after Mitch stopped playing sports and going to school. He actually feels pretty bad about that because he likes Mitch a lot and has missed him." Robin seemed excited to add to the story.

Ginny smiled. She was so happy Mitch and Josh were becoming friends again. Even if it weren't for Homecoming, and Robin and Josh liking each other, Ginny was just glad Mitch was getting his friends back.

"A couple months after Mitch's accident, my dad was launching this study about kids and computer programming. He put me in the study, but I wasn't allowed to say who I was or admit he was my dad. He didn't want the other kids to think I was getting any special treatment or anything. We all had to sign something saying we'd never share information that would give away who we are in real life. My dad was really strict about this."

Robin started picking up shoes, but kept her eyes on Ginny, captivated by the story.

Ginny continued, "He was my first partner, and I assumed he lived somewhere far away. We kept getting partnered together and became friends. Well, this went on and on, and it seemed like we really liked each other—which you guys all knew. My Sportstatsguy, kind of an online boyfriend. Last spring he told me about his podcast, which I listened to kind of as background noise. And in August, on his podcast, he said he was going back to school, and he mentioned Kenwood. I started listening more closely and realized Sportstatsguy, or *Sports with Mitch*, was Mitch Henry. I couldn't believe I hadn't figured it out sooner."

"Why didn't you tell him right away? Or, more importantly, me?" Robin held up a green high heel that was probably five inches high.

Ginny shook her head. "I was shocked and was trying to think of all the things that should have given it away in all the time we've been friends. Then, as time passed, I felt bad for knowing and not telling him, so I decided I'd tell him in person once school started."

"Hate to point out the obvious, Gin, but school started like three weeks ago." Robin held up another green shoe—this one had a pointy toe and a lower heel, and it was the exact color of green of Robin's dress. A navy one just like it sat next to where it had been on the shelf.

"Yes! That's perfect!" Ginny said, grabbing the navy heel. A salesman took the shoes, asked their sizes, and ran into the back to find shoes for both of them to try on.

"Also, I don't want to freak you out or anything, but I hear there are some girls who like Mitch."

Ginny looked up, worried. "Who?"

"I think Angie Rasmussen, for one. And then I heard some sixth graders talking about him in the hall today. I just think that you need to tell him soon," Robin said.

Ginny didn't know what to say. "Yeah, let me think about it. I'm not sure how to tell him, and it has to be done right. I don't want him to be mad."

"Ginny, do you know what this means? If you guys go to Homecoming together, we could double date!" She clapped her hands together and smiled.

Ginny raised her eyebrows and smiled back. It was everything she'd been hoping for, but she was starting to feel a little panicky. Robin was pushing her to tell Mitch the truth, and Ginny had no idea how to do that. And who were these other girls who liked Mitch? She'd never considered that as a possibility before. Her stomach started doing flips and Ginny knew she'd have to figure out a way to tell Mitch the truth. Soon.

12

MITCH

Mitch shut his history book with fifteen minutes to spare before he and Rosco were going to meet up. He opened his laptop and went to a website-building site. He started searching available names.

www.thewholetruth.com - Taken.

www.tellthewholetruth.com - Available, but $1,700 per year. Yikes.

www.thewholetruthandnothingbutthetruth.com - Taken. Also way too long.

Mitch tapped his finger on his chin. It needed to be something that was easy to remember but also went along with what the two program interruptions had been called.

www.confessions.com - Taken.

Mitch puffed his cheeks and blew air out, slumping back in his chair. He'd thought of the idea in Health class. They were on a mental health unit, and today Mr. Schmidt was talking about lying and secrets. He referenced studies on keeping secrets and telling lies and talked about the burden of holding things inside instead of talking. Mitch thought about the secrets that had been revealed on his show. They had brought in a ton of new listeners. If he was perfectly honest, they also helped him find his friends again. But he didn't feel good about outing people's secrets. He did not enjoy what happened with Becca today and he wasn't interested in having that happen with anyone else. But what if there was a way for people to tell their own secrets? A place for confessions?

He sat up in his chair and quickly typed in the search box. www.yourwholetruth.com - Available. And only $15 for a year. He filled out the information, paid, and just like that he was the proud owner of a new website. His laptop chirped.

Rosco: Hey you!

Sportstatsguy: Hey you. Okay I have a plan but I need your help. You're better at finding things than I am. I need to figure out how to make my podcast more secure so I can stop the hacking.

She didn't respond right away. Mitch was anxious to get this done, and they didn't have tons of time before his mom would be telling him to go to bed. With Rosco's dad home, she'd have an earlier bedtime too.

Rosco: You want to stop the hacking?

Sportstatsguy: Yeah. The girl whose secret was revealed last night freaked out on me. I don't want that to happen again. I feel really really bad. But I have an idea of how I can keep up the secrets theme but not get anyone in trouble or mad at me.

It took a while for her to answer again. Usually she was much more responsive. He wondered if she was hanging out with her dad or something.

Rosco: What is your idea?

Sportstatsguy: I'm setting up a website where people can tell their own secrets. Only I can access what people submit, but they will know when they do it that I might play them on my podcast. That way, I can keep my new listeners and maybe even get more, but nobody can get mad at me for the secrets that are told.

This time she responded right away.

Rosco: Genius. What can I do?

Sportstatsguy: Can you go into my podcast and figure out how someone is hacking into it and if you can stop it from happening again? I just don't know enough about that stuff to do it myself. I'm going to work on setting up the website. I even have the site name!

Rosco: What is it?

Sportstatsguy: www.yourwholetruth.com

Rosco: Well that's just brilliant. Okay, give me your password and the host site for your podcast, I'll see what I can figure out.

Sportstatsguy: Done!

■ ■ ■

After an hour, Mitch had built the website. The homepage looked like an old tattered diary. You clicked on "Enter" and the diary opened as if wind had blown the cover back, and the pages turned quickly. Then you had the option of typing out a "journal entry" or recording an audio clip. If you chose to record an audio clip, you could also choose if you wanted your voice altered or left alone. If you typed something, you could choose what voice and accent would read it if it was picked to be featured on the podcast. At the bottom of the page it would keep track of how many secrets had been submitted. It was probably the best website Mitch had ever created. Sometimes when he had way less time than he thought he needed, Mitch did something really cool. It was always that way in sports too. "Less thinking, more doing," his dad often said.

Rosco said she found the problem with the security of his podcast and fixed it. She said she could almost guarantee the show would not be hacked again and Mitch believed her.

The last thing he had to do was issue a special announcement to followers of his podcast. Before this week he had eleven followers. When he went in to make his announcement tonight, there were eighty. He recorded it quickly, knowing he was running out of time.

"Hey there, it's Mitch from *Sports with Mitch*. We're going to try something new. Instead of someone else revealing people's secrets without their permission, this is your chance to tell your own. Go to www.yourwholetruth.com and get whatever you've been holding inside off your chest. Your secret might be featured on an upcoming *Sports with Mitch* show. We'll still talk sports because there is A LOT to talk about these days, but we'll also be sharing secrets. Tune in tomorrow at eight to see what your friends have been hiding!"

He sent this to his followers, and by the time he shut his laptop there were already nineteen likes and several forwards. Word was going to get out fast.

■ ■ ■

It was late. Mitch forgot to set his alarm and woke up twenty minutes later than usual. He was starting his second Pop-Tart when he opened the door to school and pulled his headphones off so they dangled around his neck. The five-minute warning bell rang when he turned the corner to get to his locker and saw a small group in front of it. Zach and Jin were fake fighting and Josh and Taylor were talking to Robin and Ginny.

Mouth full of Pop-Tart, he nodded at everyone when he reached his locker.

"Mitch, you evil genius, you!" Jin clapped his back and they all moved back so Mitch could get into his locker.

"Because I'm eating a Pop-Tart?" Mitch asked, throwing his headphones into his locker and taking out his books. He wasn't used to talking to this many people so soon after waking up.

"Funny guy," Zach said, still trying to land fake punches on Jin's face.

"The website," Robin said. "I mean, people must have been on it all night."

Mitch shut his locker and turned around, confused. After all, he had still been in bed twenty minutes ago.

"The website you set up? Last time I checked, the counter on the bottom was at like 100," Robin continued.

"Wait, seriously?" Mitch asked, shocked. The guys started walking separate ways.

"Yes, seriously. Come on, Señorita Klein is going to make us conjugate more verbs if we're late," Jin said nodding in the direction of their first class.

Mitch followed him, stunned.

■ ■ ■

"So like, I guess what I'm asking is, what if someone submits a secret and then decides they don't want it to be on your podcast or whatever?" Mitch had barely made it out of the bathroom when two eighth grade girls stopped him. The one who was talking was chewing gum with her mouth open and was standing close enough for Mitch to smell that it was watermelon flavored. He didn't know her name but had seen her around. She had dark hair with purple streaks and wore all black. Mitch was at least four inches taller than she was but he was pretty sure she could beat him up if she wanted to.

"Ahh . . . there is a 'Contact' page, just go there and explain that you've changed . . ."

"No, it's not *me,* you moron. I'm asking for a friend."

"Right, okay, well they can say they've changed their mind. I'm not going to play secrets unless the person wants it to be public. Also, it's still a sports show, so most of the show will be about football and stuff."

"Whatever, okay. Thanks." She snapped her gum and she and her friend went into the girls' bathroom across the hall.

Before returning to band, Mitch slipped back into the bathroom. Students were supposed to leave their phones in their lockers at all times during class periods, but the suspense had been killing him all morning. He typed in www.yourwholetruth.com and when the page loaded he looked at the counter at the bottom.

"What?!" He whispered to the empty bathroom. The counter read 267 confessions. How could that many people have been to the site already? Especially since everyone he knew was in school. When would they have the chance to go online?

He stuffed his phone in his back pocket and returned to class. They were playing the end of the *Rocky* theme song. He sat and quickly found his spot in the music and joined in. The bell rang just as they were finishing the song. Everyone started packing up their instruments, and Mr. Swan started calling out announcements.

"I need you guys to be practicing thirty minutes a day. This isn't elementary school anymore, people. If you aren't willing to practice, you shouldn't be in band. Mr. Henry? Can you please stay for a couple of minutes?" Mitch looked up, surprised. Mr. Swan never asked students to stay late. What if he knew about the website? He never even thought about adults finding out. He went back to putting his sax away, trying to figure out what kind of trouble he could be in. Did Becca tell her parents? Or Principal Deeb?

Once everyone left, Mitch walked down the steps to the bottom of the room, where Mr. Swan was organizing music for his next class.

"Mitch! I want to talk to you about something, have a seat." Mr. Swan pulled a chair over and sat in another.

Mitch sat down, his mind racing. He hadn't been this scared in a long time.

"You did great in the concert last week. I was really impressed. I was picking up some supplies last night and ran into Bobby B. at his store. We talked about you. I'm wondering if you'd be willing to switch to the baritone sax?"

Mitch let out the breath he'd been holding.

"Wait, hear me out! I'd like you to think about switching to the bari sax because we need one or two in each grade to have a well-rounded band. But I'm also wondering if you'd be interested in joining the high school jazz ensemble. I have one senior and one junior that play the bari, but after that I've got nobody. I need a succession plan and I think you might be it."

Mitch's stomach filled with butterflies. The jazz ensemble at Kenwood High School was an award-winning group. Mitch's mom loved jazz, so he'd been listening to it all of his life. This was a big deal.

"Do I need to try out or something? How does that work?"

Mr. Swan smiled and nodded. "I'd like to send you home with a bari sax today and have you try using it for a few days to get a feel for it. If you hate it, we'll keep you on the alto sax. But if you think you might like it and are willing to give it a shot,

I'll work with Bobby B. to change your rental agreement and we'll go from there. I'd have you sit in with the jazz ensemble at the high school as early as next week."

"Yeah, okay, let's do it!" agreed Mitch. Mr. Swan stood and went over to large blue metal shelves that held all sorts of instrument cases. He bent and pulled out a large case from the bottom shelf.

"It's a lot bigger. Why don't you stop here after school so you don't have to figure out where to put this now?"

"Okay. Thanks, Mr. Swan!" Mitch left the band room and jogged to the cafeteria. His parents were going to be so excited and proud.

13

GINNY

"Candlestick!"
   "High V!"
   "T!"
   "Low V!"
   "T!"
   "High V!"
   "Candlestick!"
Sophia Von Ulm yelled instructions from the front of the gym and the high school and junior high squads followed. Thursday practices involved precision drills and weight training. Ginny was always amazed at how sore her arms were at the end of Thursday practice. Simply from doing four moves, over and over again, with weights.

   "Remember your knuckles should be facing up for all of these positions except candlesticks, then the top of your thumbs should be up. Let's go again. Candlestick . . ."

Ginny couldn't concentrate. Thoughts of Mitch and her dad jumbled together. Dad came home only two days ago, and the difference in how Ginny felt was huge. She slept better, she was more relaxed, and she felt almost carefree. It was like a weight had been lifted from her shoulders. She wanted to live with him. At least part of the time. But he was a professor at a prestigious college in Chicago, and she couldn't move to Chicago, not with all of her friends, her mom, and Mitch in Minnesota. Dad was in charge of his entire department. He couldn't give that up to move home. If only he could move back to Minnesota so Ginny could live with him some of the time.

And then there was Mitch. She felt closer to him than ever, but the thought of telling him who she really was made her stomach turn. What if he was angry that she'd kept it a secret for so many months? What if he stopped talking to her? What if she didn't tell him soon enough and he started liking another girl? She *had* to tell him. Today, if possible. But she just couldn't! The risks were too high.

She didn't want her dad to leave. She didn't want Mitch to be mad. Her mind was racing with thoughts of her dad, Mitch, the navy dress sitting on hold at Juju's, even just cheerleading and school. There was so much going on that she felt frazzled, which was unusual for her.

"Ladies, we need to be sharper than this with our movements, let's go!"

"Gin," Alicia whispered from behind Ginny. "I think she's talking to us, you okay?"

Ginny nodded and tried to focus on keeping her arms straight and her movements sharp and precise.

"Okay, let's move on to jumps. I'll give you five minutes to stretch and grab a drink."

Ginny pulled her right heel up to the back of her thigh, held it in place for twenty seconds, and then switched to her left leg.

"Okay, what's going on?" Alicia put her hand on Ginny's shoulder to balance while she too stood on one leg, stretching the other. "Come on, spill."

"I just," Ginny started. She looked down and shook her head, not really knowing where to start. She wasn't ready to tell Alicia about Mitch. Not yet.

Alicia switched legs and used Ginny's other shoulder for balance. "Gin, what is it?"

"I think I want to live with my dad." Saying it out loud felt good. She'd thought it a million times but she'd never actually said the words to anyone.

"You want to move to Chicago?"

"No, I mean I want him to come back and live somewhere around here. Maybe I could live part-time with my mom and part-time with my dad?"

Alicia cocked her head to the side. "Have you talked to him or your mom about this?"

The music started and Alicia squeezed Ginny's arm before going back to her spot.

"Five, six, seven, eight, toe touch, pike, toe touch . . ."

Ginny did her jumps and thought about Alicia's question. She hadn't ever asked her mom or her dad if there was a way to live with both of them. She always assumed it was out of the question. She definitely never brought it up with mom because she knew her mother would get mad. It seemed like Mom *liked* having Ginny all to herself, even though she was gone so much of the time.

■ ■ ■

An hour later, muscles burning and soaked with sweat, Alicia and Ginny slowly walked through the mostly empty halls to the front of the school. Alicia's older sister Mindi, a varsity hockey cheerleader, was waiting for her at the front door, dramatically tapping the face of her watch.

"I've gotta go, apparently someone is in a hurry. But Gin, if you don't ask, the answer will always be no. And who knows, it might be no anyway, but what if they said yes?" She smiled at Ginny and her brown eyes sparkled.

Ginny squeezed her in a quick, sweaty hug. "Thanks, Alicia."

Alicia ran ahead and called over her shoulder, "Hey, your dad is out here in your mom's car!"

Ginny jogged to the door and saw Mom's SUV with the LISBETH license plate, Dad in the driver's seat and Lucky in the passenger seat. She chuckled, ran outside, and opened the door. Lucky jumped to the back seat and Ginny crawled in.

"I'm not sure what you and Mom have been eating, but there weren't ingredients to make hardly anything, let alone pizza."

"Pizza? YES!!!" Ginny loved Dad's homemade pizza. It was legendary.

Dad pulled out of the junior high lot toward home. "Pizza tomorrow night! What do we have for homework?"

"Algebra, English, and I think that's it." Ginny hit the seat warmer button and waited for the warmth to envelop her. She looked over at Dad again, realizing he was wearing a suit and tie. Usually he was in jeans, a sweatshirt or track jacket, and funky tennis shoes.

"Why are you dressed up?"

"I had a couple of meetings today," he said, turning onto their street.

Ginny wondered what kind of meetings he could be having in Minnesota.

"Help me unload the groceries, then you can work on your homework while I make dinner."

Ginny threw her backpack and cheerleading bag inside the house and then helped bring in the bags of groceries. It took four trips each for them to get all the bags inside. She didn't think there had been this much food in the house since Dad left. Mom had a couple of signature dishes but mostly, they ate really easy stuff or went out to dinner. A lot of the time, Ginny fed herself, because Mom was gone or busy doing something.

"How about we to go to Book Nook after dinner? I have some books I need to pick up," Dad said, filling the fridge with meat and cheese.

Ginny passed him a box of applesauce pouches. "And hot chocolate at The Drip?"

"Obviously," Dad said. Ginny smiled.

■ ■ ■

Dad held the heavy door to Book Nook and Ginny walked in under his outstretched arm, holding onto her hot chocolate with both hands to keep them warm. The smell of books, leather, and furniture cleaner welcomed her like an old friend. She'd been here only a few days ago, but it felt different when she was with Dad. Everything felt different with Dad. It was like she belonged somewhere, everywhere, instead of feeling alone.

"Mr. Ross! You're back in town!" Pete came out from around the front counter and shook Dad's hand. Ginny gave him a dirty look. What was she? Chopped liver? "And Ginny, you're still *in* town," Pete said dryly, and shook his head in mock disappointment.

"Don't you ever go to school?" Ginny asked, walking straight back to the mystery section of the store. She knew that, with Dad, she'd be able to get a couple of books out of this trip.

"Touche!" Pete called after her. Then, quieter, he said, "I have the books you called about behind the counter. Let's take a look and see if they will work."

Ginny glanced back and saw Dad and Pete bent over the counter, looking at a book on top of a stack of several. She couldn't be sure but she was starting to think Dad was up to something. Meetings in town, ordering books from Book Nook when he had an entire university book store at his disposal in Chicago, and stocking the house with enough food to last far longer than the number of days he'd be staying.

Ginny took a sip of her hot chocolate and found the "K" section. She slid her pointer finger over the spines of Stephen

King books she'd already read until she reached one she hadn't. She pulled it out and skimmed the synopsis on the back.

"Yikes," she said quietly, tucking it under her arm. It sounded scary but in the best way possible. She continued to grab books and, when she'd collected four, returned to the front where Dad and Pete still stood.

"Dad, which of these am I old enough for?" She wasn't allowed to get just any Stephen King books—she was only thirteen, after all—but Dad had read all of them and could always tell her which ones might be inappropriate or even too scary.

She set her drink on the counter and held them up one at a time, and Dad said, "Yes, no, absolutely not, yes." Two out of four wasn't bad. She set the two he okayed next to his stack of books and walked back to return the two Dad vetoed.

When she got back to the front, the books were all in a deep-blue paper bag that said Book Nook in cream-colored calligraphy on the front.

"I'll send you the information, Pete. It might be a really great program for you, and the application deadline is coming right up."

"Thanks, Mr. Ross, that'd be great." He waved and Ginny followed Dad out the front door and toward The Drip.

"What is he talking about?" Ginny asked as they walked.

"Pete is looking at graduate programs because he's done with college in the spring. I'm sending him information on a program that I think would be great for him."

"One of yours?" Ginny asked, trying to get an idea of what was going on. She didn't know what was stopping her from just asking him.

"Yep, now let's get home. I want to go for a run with Lucky before it's too dark."

Ginny needed to shower and then she had to listen to Mitch's podcast. She didn't have to come up with a new hack, at least not for now, which was kind of a relief. She wasn't positive she wouldn't need to use that trick again, but while Dad was here she didn't want to have to worry about finding more juicy secrets to expose. With Dad home, she could barely be sure to listen to Mitch's podcast, let alone hack into it with more secrets. Mitch had taken over the reins with what, she had to admit, was a really good plan.

Dad being home also allowed Ginny to put off telling Mitch who she was. She could avoid it, but she was starting to feel a pit in her stomach that never seemed to go away. She knew she had to tell him, of course she knew that, but the longer she waited the more worried she was about how he'd react. She honestly couldn't decide what was worse, not knowing how he would take the truth, or just never telling him and liking him from the sidelines. Either way, Ginny had to make a decision and do something, or it might drive her crazy.

14

MITCH

The secrets Mitch listened to were heartbreaking. One girl said that she didn't feel like anyone at home loved her and that she felt all alone. Another said she had never been able to read but was too embarrassed to ask for help. A boy said he'd always felt like he was supposed to be a girl but that his parents didn't understand and punished him when he tried on dresses or asked people to call him by a different name.

Mitch stared at the screen of his laptop with a lump in his throat. The melancholy song his sister was practicing on the piano didn't help, but the secrets he'd listened to thus far were so sad. He stood up and went to his window, where he could see a few teams still practicing under the lights surrounding the athletic fields.

He could lose his podcast and not be able to play sports for the rest of his life and he'd still be luckier than a whole lot of kids. He stood with his arms crossed watching the little soccer players run after the ball. Some players sat down

THE WHOLE TRUTH 103

in the middle of the field and pulled grass, not paying attention to the game around them. The kids couldn't be older than five or six. Usually, watching kids play out there made Mitch jealous and a little resentful. Today, however, he felt lucky.

Mitch felt simultaneously grateful for his own life and so sad for these kids who didn't have the support of their family or the same abilities that he had. He couldn't fathom being in any of the situations that he'd listened to. He wondered how many of them went to Kenwood Junior High. He even tried to think of ways to find out who they were so he could try to help. Or at least be a friend to them.

He went back to his desk and scrolled through the growing list of audio files. He had to pick one or two to play on his show but he didn't feel comfortable exposing people who were already suffering. He needed advice.

Sportstatsguy: Hey you, do you have a second?

Rosco: Hey you, what's up? Almost show time!

Sportstatsguy: I set up that website and there are already three hundred secrets.

Rosco: Oh my gosh that's awesome!

Sportstatsguy: I guess...but the ones I've listened to are really sad. Like, REALLY sad.

Rosco: You put something on the site that says the secrets might be played on your podcast, right?

Sportstatsguy: Yeah, I mean that's the point, but wouldn't it be hard to hear your secret on a podcast? It would be so embarrassing.

Rosco: Maybe. But what if it made other people who are having the same kinds of problems feel like they aren't the only ones?

Mitch thought about that. Rosco was right, it could make other people feel better about their own situations.

Sportstatsguy: You're right. Okay, I have to pick a couple and then it's time for the show. Will you listen?
Rosco: Of course!

■ ■ ■

"Welcome to the Thursday edition of *Sports with Mitch*. Tonight we're going to talk about baseball. The season is wrapping up and I want predictions and I want someone to tell me the Cubs are going to be World Series Champions again. First, as you know, someone has been exposing secrets on the last couple episodes of this podcast. I think I've fixed that, but I also set up a place for all of you to tell your own secrets. It turns out a lot of you had things to say. I'll play a couple on each show and you can call in if you want to comment, but keep the mean stuff to yourselves."

Mitch clicked on the first clip. He closed his eyes and held his breath.

"Hi. I'm in seventh grade and I can't really read. I mean, I can read words by themselves if they aren't too long. But I can't read books, or letters, or notes. It's hard for me to focus on each word. My parents have gotten me glasses to help, but they don't really. And I think they've just accepted the fact that I'm dumb. I really don't think I'm dumb, but I'm so embarrassed. I should have asked for help a long time ago, but I just thought it would get better. Well, now I'm thirteen and I can't read. I just don't know what to do or who to even talk to. Okay, thanks."

Calls started buzzing before the clip was even done. Mitch let out his breath and clicked on a call.

"Hey, you're on *Sports with Mitch*. Are you calling to tell me the Cubs are going to the World Series?"

"Naw, man, you're delusional. Seriously. But I wanted to tell the girl who can't read that she might be dyslexic. Like me. I felt exactly like this until I talked to a specialist who helped me. And that was when I was in ninth grade, so I was even older than she is. Go to your school counselor. They will help you. Oh, and Mitch?"

"Yeah?"

"You'd be better off rooting for the Yankees." The caller laughed out loud and hung up. Anyone who listened to Mitch's show knew he *hated* the Yankees.

"Yeah, *that's* never gonna happen. Next caller?"

"I just want to tell that girl that she's really brave and that I agree with your last caller. She's not dumb, it's gotta be something else."

"Thanks for the call." Mitch took several more, a mix of support for the girl who told her secret and sports talk. Then he switched to talking about high school sports.

It was the most popular show he ever had. Halfway through, he checked the number of listeners, and there were

163. He felt light-headed. He couldn't believe that this was happening. But something nagged at him that he couldn't put his finger on.

With just a few minutes left in the show, he got the next secret ready. He decided that one secret could be sad but the second one had to be funny, or embarrassing, but not depressing.

"Before I leave you tonight, one more secret. I hope you'll join me again on Sunday night!"

"Hi. So I have the biggest crush on Jin Zhao," the clip started. Mitch couldn't keep from laughing. Jin was going to freak out. "I mean, I know he's super goofy, but he's so funny. I went to some of his baseball games last year and I've seen him at robotics competitions. He's so cute! I want to ask him to Homecoming, but I'm pretty sure he doesn't even know I exist. Anyway, if you're listening, Jin, I think you're awesome!" The clip ended with giggling and Mitch smiled. He knew it would be a matter of seconds before his phone started buzzing.

■ ■ ■

Mitch was deep in thought as he walked into school the next morning, trying to calculate how much of last night's show was sports-related and how much was secret-related. While the increase in listeners was exciting, the decrease in the sports part troubled him. He turned the corner and stopped, forcing anyone walking behind him to sidestep to avoid running into him. The hallway in front of his locker was like a circus. He thought he could see Josh and Robin, but other than that there were people from all three grades in front of his locker.

"Ginny, it's you, isn't it? Yes, I will go out with you," Jin said as Mitch reached the group.

"Wrong," Ginny responded, laughing. Mitch liked her laugh. It reminded him of his mom's.

He nudged Jin to get out of the way so he could open his locker. "Haven't found her yet?"

"Mitchell, you need to help me. The dance is a week away and I'll need to look on point."

"We wouldn't want Jin to not look 'on point,'" Ginny joked, making the quotation motions with her fingers. She was funny too.

Mitch looked around at the other people standing around.

" . . . felt so bad! I mean, how awful to have to pretend, right?"

" . . . I submitted a secret yesterday, but I don't think it's juicy enough for . . ."

" . . . think Jin is cute too, for an eighth grader . . ."

Mitch didn't know half of the people talking around him. And it was weird, they were kind of talking about him, but none of them were really talking *to* him.

The five-minute warning bell rang and the crowd scattered.

Jin started walking, still talking about his mystery woman. "I feel like there is a real possibility that she's in our Spanish class. You need to keep a watch out for anyone staring at me adoringly."

Mitch shook his head and rolled his eyes. "You got it, buddy."

He and Jin were friends before Mom pulled him out of school, but eighth grade Jin was much funnier and more outgoing than he was in sixth grade. Back then he was kind of quiet.

A group of girls passed them and said, "Hi, Mitch!" in unison. Mitch turned around and watched them walk away.

"*Hi, Mitch,*" Jin repeated in a high voice.

"I don't even know who those girls are," Mitch admitted.

"You're a star now, baby. Better get used to it!"

As he followed Jin into first period he realized that a week ago, he had been a loner. He and Josh were starting to talk more but he didn't have a group of friends. He didn't have plans to hang out with anybody. And now he sat with these guys at lunch, they texted him, he and Josh were becoming friends like they used to be. He even had girls talking to him. He finally felt like he belonged here, instead of feeling like an outsider. All because of his podcast. The one he might lose.

15

GINNY

The sleepover was Dad's idea. They were eating breakfast before Ginny left for school, and he offered to make pizza if Ginny wanted to invite her friends over after school. He would take them to the football game and bring them back to their house to spend the night. Ginny hadn't had her friends sleep over in a long time. Often, she was home with Grandma, and Ginny was too embarrassed to subject her friends to an evening with her. When Mom was home she always made such a big deal of spending time together that Ginny didn't even ask if she could have friends over. The only time she got to do sleepovers was when her mom was traveling and Grandma couldn't come over. Then she'd get to go spend the night with one of her friends.

It had been a good day. School was buzzing about Mitch's new secrets website, Mitch seemed happy, and she knew he was having the guys over tonight too, which was a big deal for him. It felt like it was all coming together.

Ginny didn't even think she'd need to hack into his show again. He'd come up with his own way of getting people to listen. Her plan had worked. She couldn't believe it had worked out so perfectly.

"Who do you think likes Jin?" Emily asked as they walked down Virginia Avenue toward Ginny's house.

"He's hard not to like," Alicia offered. Ginny, Robin, and Emily stopped and looked at her quizzically. "What? No, it wasn't *me*, I'm just saying, he *is* pretty funny."

The girls started walking again, kicking piles of leaves as they went. Ginny wanted to tell Alicia and Emily about Mitch. She'd been thinking about it all day. She was so tired of keeping secrets. Not that she would tell them about the hacking. No, if she told anyone about that she would have to tell Mitch himself. But it wouldn't hurt to admit she *liked* him. And that he was the online friend she'd been telling them about for all of these months. Ginny trusted them and knew they wouldn't tell her secret.

"You could ask Jin to the dance," Robin said, interrupting Ginny's thinking. "I mean, it's not like the girl who likes him is going to. Nobody knows who she is."

Ginny could tell Alicia was thinking about it. They turned into her driveway and Alicia said, "Yeah, but that would be mean. We all know she's out there and likes him."

"Yeah, but," Emily echoed, "unlike the mystery girl, you actually know him and he knows who you are."

Ginny's mind was suddenly filled with ideas about going to the dance with Mitch and both her friends and his. Her thoughts were interrupted by Lucky barking his hellos.

Robin bent to let Lucky lick her chin. "We'll see them at the game tonight," she said as she dried her chin with the sleeve of her fleece. "They are going to Mitch's for dinner before the game."

Robin eyed Ginny. Ginny took her turn greeting Lucky, ignoring Robin's obvious nudge to tell Alicia and Emily about Mitch.

When they opened the front door, smells of baking crust, garlic, and basil wafted from the kitchen.

"I have been excited about your dad's pizza all day," Alicia admitted.

They dropped their bags at the bottom of the stairs and followed their noses to the kitchen.

"Ladies! I hope you're hungry, I have three pizzas baking." Dad was wearing a ruffled apron that was far too small for his large frame.

They all nodded, as if in a hunger-induced trance.

"Let's go downstairs and make up our beds for later," said Ginny, breaking the spell.

The basement was made for having people over. Ginny rarely went down there anymore, but they used to have parties that filled the main floor with adults and the kids were always sent to the basement. They had a skee-ball machine, a Ms. Pac-Man video game, and a big TV. The u-shaped couch was still big enough to hold all four girls lying down. As the girls chose their spots and started making their beds, Ginny realized that being in the basement felt like going back in time. She and her mom never came downstairs. From time to time Ginny would play a game of Ms. Pac-Man, but that was the only time she went down there.

"So Gin, is there anyone you would want to ask to the dan—" Robin started. She was interrupted by Dad's booming voice.

"Tha pizza is-a ready!" he exclaimed in a mock Italian accent.

The girls dropped the blankets and pillows they were organizing and ran for the stairs.

■ ■ ■

"Thanks, Leo," the girls called in unison as they spilled out of Ginny's mom's car.

"I'll be back at nine," he called after them.

Ginny scanned the lines of people waiting to buy tickets but didn't see Mitch, or the other guys.

"They're already in the stands," Robin whispered.

Ginny loved that Robin could read her mind sometimes. She leaned her head to touch Robin's and then they walked to the ticket counters.

It was a chilly night. All four girls were wearing some sort of fleece or jacket for their sports teams, and stretchy gloves. They stood in the concessions line for what seemed like forever and finally, when all four of them had large whipped cream-topped hot chocolates in their hands, they started walking toward the stands.

"Hey, I see the guys," Alicia said, pointing to the front row at the far end of the bleachers. Most sections were filled with high school kids or parents from Kenwood or St. Mary's, the opposing team. A very small number of junior high kids were there.

Robin, who had been texting and walking, looked up and waved at Josh, who was standing up and searching the crowd. He waved back when he spotted her and motioned for them to join them.

Ginny could see Mitch talking to a boy in a baseball cap that she didn't recognize. Her stomach flipped. The mixing of her worlds, online and real, was getting confusing. She was starting to have trouble remembering who knew what. She didn't want Mitch to know too much about her in real life, because he was smart enough to figure out she had a lot in common with his other friend, Rosco. She tightened her grip on her hot chocolate to try to slow her racing mind as they climbed the bleacher stairs. "I *have* to tell him," she thought as they neared the boys.

"Hello, ladies!" Jin called out.

The girls filed into the row behind them. When Ginny sat down she realized the person she'd seen Mitch talking to had a thick and curly mane of brown hair flowing from the back of the baseball cap, and that it wasn't a boy at all. She inhaled sharply and then quickly started coughing to disguise her reaction. Ginny thought the girl looked familiar but she wasn't sure who she was. Mitch and the girl started laughing, hard. Ginny felt her phone vibrate and pulled it out of her pocket with her gloved hand.

Robin Blair - 7:34pm: Who's that girl?

Ginny, holding her hot chocolate in her left hand, used her teeth to pull off her glove and texted back:

Ginny Ross - 7:35pm: I don't know? I think I've seen her before but I'm not sure where.

She looked up at Robin, who was eyeing the girl critically.

"Do you guys know Samantha Rasmussen?" asked Josh.

The girl Mitch was talking to looked up at the mention of her name and turned around to face the girls. Mitch turned around too. He smiled and waved at them.

"Hi," said Samantha. "I'm Sam, I go to St. Mary's." She gave them a genuine smile that made her eyes sparkle. They were the bluest eyes Ginny had ever seen. Her skin was light and she had freckles on her cheeks. She was impossibly pretty and Ginny felt her chest tighten.

"Sam's little sister and my little sister are best friends," Mitch explained, "and her brother is the quarterback for St. Mary's." Mitch gestured to the field.

"And she was in our kindergarten class," added Josh.

Ginny then knew why she looked so familiar. Sam went to their elementary school with them for the first two years. Ginny had never been friends with her because they never in the same class, but she remembered her. She used to have thick glasses and short hair.

"Hi," Emily said. "I'm Emily. This is Alicia, Robin, and Ginny."

"I remember you guys," said Sam, "but nice to meet you again." There was a loud cheer around them and everyone's attention turned back to the field. Someone made a touchdown and the school song started playing loudly over the PA. After that Mitch and Sam went back to talking to each other.

Ginny felt frozen. She didn't know what to do. She returned her phone to her pocket and focused on her hot chocolate while her friends talked to the boys.

"It's just so crazy," Ginny heard Sam say. "I mean, how can all these people have such juicy secrets?"

Ginny started arguing with herself in her head. 'Tell him, don't tell him, I have to tell him, I can't tell him, but I have to, but I can't . . .' She realized she had to say something or she might die, or people would notice her unusual silence. "Jin, any luck finding your mystery woman?" she asked.

Josh and Zach, who sat on either side of Jin, elbowed him and laughed. Jin looked back at the girls, making a point to look each one of them in the eye. "I'm assuming," he said and then paused dramatically, "it's one of you." He paused again and put his hand to his heart. "And I just want to say, yes, I'll go to Homecoming with you."

This made everyone laugh. Even Ginny cracked a smile.

"You are completely ridiculous," Alicia said, still laughing. Ginny could tell that Alicia liked him more than she was willing to admit.

"It's not one of us," Robin said, shaking her head.

"Well, I should tell you, I would still go to Homecoming with any of you. Well, not *you,* Robin. Obviously."

When Josh started commenting on the game, and the boys turned back to the field, Ginny, Robin, and Emily looked at Alicia pointedly. She was looking straight ahead, but her cheeks were pink with embarrassment and her lips were pursed as she tried to hide her smile.

"I should go back and sit with my parents," Sam said, standing up. Everyone said goodbye and waved. She adjusted her baseball hat and said, "I'll see you later, Mitch." Mitch nodded, smiling.

When she'd disappeared into the crowd, Taylor turned to Mitch and said, "That girl got *cute*! She did not look like that before."

Josh laughed. "Last time we saw her, we didn't think *any* girls were cute, remember?"

Ginny stood suddenly, almost losing grip of what was left of her hot chocolate. "I'm running to the bathroom," she whispered to her friends.

Robin stood. "I'll go with you."

Ginny quickly made her way for the stairs with Robin trying to catch up behind her. She felt panicky. Soon she felt Robin gripping her arm above her elbow and it calmed her a little.

When they got to the bathroom, Robin pulled Ginny into one of the larger stalls. Ginny started to pace the small space and finally stopped, facing Robin. "What did she mean, she'd see Mitch later?"

"Gin, everyone says 'see you later.'" Ginny was shaking her head before Robin had even finished her sentence.

"But why did she say it to Mitch specifically?" She looked at Robin with pleading eyes. She wanted Robin to make her feel better. To assure her that she hadn't seen what Ginny had seen.

Robin sighed. "Well, probably because he's the only one she actually knows? But, Ginny," she said looking at Ginny sternly, "if you don't tell Mitch who you are, someone else might try to get him."

Ginny looked down. She'd never considered it as an option. Just a week or so ago, Mitch was a loner with barely any friends. Now there were pretty girls from different schools talking to him and listening to his podcast. She would have to do something.

She stood up straighter and opened the stall door, walking to the mirrors that lined the wall above the sinks. "Okay, I'm going to have to make him notice me now." She pulled out lip gloss and spread it across her lips.

Robin smiled, and looked in the mirror next to Ginny. "Good, now let's go. We have an hour and a half before your dad comes. Plenty of time to make an impression. Or," Robin paused, "you could just *tell him who you are.*"

Ginny nodded at her reflection and took Robin by the arm. "Let's go make an impression." Robin shrugged and they walked back into the crisp fall night.

16

MITCH

Mitch checked to be sure he had everything he needed to do leaf service for the Rosses and the Stegoras. Rake, lawn bags, and his weedwacker to clean up the edges of both lawns. He started his mower and made his way to Virginia Avenue. His front right pocket vibrated and he pulled out his phone at the next stop sign.

Sam Rasmussen - 10:17am: Hey! Do you want to take our sisters to a movie this weekend?

Mitch cut the engine. He and Sam had put their numbers into each other's phones the night before, but he didn't actually think she would text him. Putting numbers in someone else's phone was just something that girls did when they met new people or made new friends.

Mitch Henry - 10:17am: I can't today. I have to rake and bag leaves at two houses then family stuff. Maybe tomorrow?

Sam Rasmussen - 10:18am: Text me tomorrow! Have a good day!

Mitch was dumbfounded. It would never have occurred to him that Sam might like *him*. He wasn't even sure how he felt about *her*.

Mitch Henry - 10:19am: Thx you too.

He put his phone back in his pocket and restarted the mower. As he drove he thought about the night before. He and the guys were in the concession line behind Sam's family. Mitch said hi to her mom and then they all started talking. Addie and Sam's sister Julia had been friends since pre-school. He knew Sam from elementary school and would see her when his family dropped Addie off at the Rasmussen house or when Julia was being dropped at his house. Sometimes their moms would start talking, and Mitch and Sam found themselves stuck having to make conversation with each other.

But Sam wasn't the only girl Mitch talked to last night. He and Ginny Ross talked quite a bit. There was just something about her. It wasn't anything different, it felt more like a recognition. She'd looked really pretty, but she always had been. Last night she was funny, and charming, but he felt comfortable with her like he did with the guys, for no good reason. It's not like they'd ever been good friends, but it *felt* like they had been last night. He didn't feel like he had to be anything but himself when he talked to her. At the end of the night, instead of thinking about messaging Rosco like he normally did, Mitch found himself replaying his conversations with Ginny.

When Mitch turned onto Virginia Avenue he was surprised to see people raking in the Rosses front yard. As he got closer, he realized it was Ginny, Robin, Alicia, and Emily. He squinted and saw that Ginny's dad was also there. His stomach flipped and he put one hand to his head to comb his fingers through his hair.

Mitch pulled in front of the lawn and cut the engine, taking a deep breath as he did so.

Mr. Ross leaned his own rake against the house and walked toward Mitch. "Young Mitchel Henry!" he bellowed. The girls looked up, taking advantage of the break.

"Hey, Mr. Ross," Mitch said getting off the mower and holding out his hand. Mr. Ross shook it. "I was scheduled to do leaf service here today."

Mr. Ross's smile faltered slightly. "I decided this morning that these girls could use a good day of working outside." He looked behind him and the girls all returned their focus to raking. "I'm not sure they're the best rakers and baggers around. Would you mind having assistants? We'll still pay your fee, of course."

Mitch shifted his weight, a little uncomfortable with the idea of having these four girls assist him. He liked working alone, but Mr. Ross was always so friendly and he didn't want to disappoint him. "Sure, that'd be great," Mitch said, giving him a smile.

"Girls, you have a new boss! I'm heading inside to get a little work done." Mr. Ross started walking toward the house and yelled, "Mr. Henry, they're all yours!"

The four girls looked at him expectantly, hints of smiles on all of their faces. Robin spoke first: "What do you want us to do, boss?"

Mitch laughed, nervously. He knew, however, that with the help of the girls he might be able to get home in time to catch some college football. Or, he guessed, maybe a movie with his sister and Sam. He stood taller and addressed the girls. "We're going to divide the lawn into pieces. Alicia and Ginny, you stay where you are. Robin, you go over to where Emily is." Mitch drew lines with his fingers to indicate the outlines of their assigned space. "Rake it into piles and I will come around to bag it. When you're done with your spot, I'll move you to the next. Deal?"

"Deal!" they said in unison.

Mitch had expected at least a little pushback, or sarcasm, but the girls were back to raking. He wondered if Mr. Ross had promised them some reward for doing yard work. He pulled the box of yard bags from his mower and jogged back to where Ginny and Alicia were raking. "So, what did your dad promise to get you all to do yard work?" Mitch asked as he started stuffing leaves from the pile into the oversized black garbage bags.

Ginny looked up. "What makes you think he had to bribe us?" The other girls laughed.

"Because," said Alicia, not even looking up from her raking, "he's met us."

"There is a movie at the end of this leafy tunnel," explained Robin.

Mitch immediately thought of Sam. He did not want to be at the same movie with Sam and their little sisters, and these girls. He couldn't even put his finger on why that was.

He tied the top of a bag, already stuffed full of red and orange leaves. "Just a movie?" Mitch asked, smiling at them.

"Oh, man," Alicia said, this time resting her chin on the wooden handle of her rake. "He knows us better than we thought."

"There may have been some treats offered," Ginny admitted.

Ginny's hair was up on top of her head but there were blonde curls that had escaped, hanging around her face. Mitch found himself wondering if *she* liked anyone. He quickly looked away, worried he'd been looking at her for too long. "Treats and a movie," Mitch said, raking leaves into a new bag. "Sounds like a good trade to me. And I'm always happy to have assistants."

He continued to work alongside the girls, directing them when needed, but mostly trying to slow his racing mind. His thoughts kept going back to Rosco. That was the real reason he felt weird about going anywhere with Sam. Then, there was his changing feelings for Ginny. What he really needed to be focusing on was his podcast. Not girls. He shook his head and tossed another full bag onto the pile that had accumulated on the Rosses' driveway.

"Are you shaking your head at *us*?" asked Robin, hand on her hip. "Are we going too slow for you?"

Mitch didn't even realize he'd shaken his head. "What? No," he said, embarrassed. "I was just," he paused, deciding what to say, "thinking." He looked at the front yard, which was almost completely raked. The girls' help cut at least two hours off his time. "You guys have saved me a ton of time," he continued.

"And *you*," said Ginny, "have made it so we can go to the movies *and* get popcorn and candy."

Ginny smiled at him and it made his stomach flip, *again*. What in the world was happening to him?

Mitch blurted out a combination of "thank you" and "you're welcome" that sounded like "thank yelcome." The girls giggled and started picking up the yard. They told him they'd finish up if he wanted to start next door and began moving the bulging bags of leaves to the end of the driveway.

Mitch quickly put his tools back on his mower and hopped on. He waved at the girls, who yelled "bye," and drove the short distance to the Stegoras' yard next door. He had no idea what to do about any of the things on his mind, but he felt confused and excited all at the same time.

■ ■ ■

One thing mom was insistent upon was volunteering. She and Dad both volunteered their time to a number of nonprofit organizations, and Mitch and Addie were expected to help at least once a month. Sometimes they served meals at homeless shelters, others they packed food to be sent to third world countries, and others still they volunteered in one of the many local food shelves.

Mitch was the last one ready because when he got home from six hours of raking and bagging leaves he and Dad watched football. Leaving him to shower at the last minute. He climbed into the back seat of the car and Dad put it in reverse.

"What is that smell?" Addie asked, her nose scrunched up in disgust.

Mitch, who had just sprayed on cologne for maybe the second or third time in his life, mumbled, "It's me."

"What do you *mean* it's *you*?" By now Addie was pinching her nose with her thumb and pointer finger.

"Adelaide," Mom said sternly as she turned around from the front seat, "come on. Enough. It smells great." She looked at Mitch and whispered, "Maybe just a little less next time, okay, honey?"

Mitch nodded, embarrassed, and quickly looked out the window. Tonight they were going to help sort through donated items that would be set out for clients of an organization that helped people get back on their feet after tragedies. It was organized by people at church and there were a lot of people from school that went to their church. Mitch knew it was possible that he'd run into someone he knew. Which is why he'd decided, before leaving his room, to spray some cologne on his clothes. He pulled off his fleece and set it between him and Addie.

Mitch could feel her looking at him. He turned to see Addie smirking.

"What?" he asked, knowing he was going to be irritated with whatever came out of her mouth.

Her smirk turned into a grin. "I saw Julia at soccer today," she said in a sing-songy voice.

Mitch knew where this was going but didn't want to give her the satisfaction. "And?" He asked, giving her a steely look, not daring to blink first.

Addie, not to be deterred *ever*, continued. "And she said you sat with Sam at the game last night."

Mom turned around at the mention of Sam's name. "You saw Sam last night?"

Mitch held his gaze at Addie until she finally blinked first, and then turned to Mom. "I saw the whole family. They're at every game, obviously."

Mom smiled and turned back toward the front. "How is Sam?"

Mitch heard Addie giggle, although she was trying to do it quietly.

"Fine, I guess. She came and sat with us for like ten minutes."

Dad glanced back and said, "I always liked her." He winked at Mitch.

"Well, *she* likes *Mitch*," Addie blurted. She'd clearly been waiting to spit that out since she brought it up.

Both Mom and Dad started laughing. Mitch knew they were laughing at how ridiculous Addie sounded, but he was annoyed. "Yeah, okay, Addie. Like you would know."

This offended her. "I *do* know. Julia told me!"

Mitch knew arguing with her would only make things worse. It was far more effective to ignore her. She hated that. He looked out the window and said nothing more while Addie tried to convince everyone in the car that her information was correct. She got more and more worked up as Mitch remained silent.

Dad pulled into a parking spot and once the car was in park he turned around. "Addie, we believe you. Thanks for sharing today's breaking news. Now can we please move on?" This shut her up, finally, and they all got out of the car and walked to the entrance of the large stone and glass building.

■ ■ ■

Mitch worked with Dad, and Addie, thankfully, stayed close to Mom. They sorted used clothes, newly purchased diapers, underwear and socks, and lightly used winter coats into sections. After four hours, the large room that normally served as the building cafeteria looked like any store you'd find in a mall. Each section had items for different age groups. Clients would arrive early the next morning to shop for their families.

When they walked out into the crisp evening air three hours later, Mitch's mood had improved considerably. "Hey," he said. "Can we go to The Drip?"

His parents and Addie were walking ahead of him, all holding hands. Addie started skipping and begged, "Please, please, please?"

Dad stopped, waiting for Mitch to catch up, and put his arm around his shoulders. "Seems like we should let a couple more people smell our boy tonight. He smells *good!*" Mitch tried to pull away but Dad tightened his grip and kissed Mitch on the top of his head.

■ ■ ■

The Drip was crowded, as it was most weekend nights. It was the turn of the season, which meant half of the people were there getting hot drinks while the others were still getting ice cream even though it was starting to get cold out.

They got in line and Mitch could see that both Rachel and Julie were working. He and his mom used to go to The Drip in the mornings. Mom would get coffee, he would get hot chocolate, she would study her law books, and Mitch would read whatever she was having him read at the time. Rachel and Julie were always so cheery and fun. Mitch was standing on his tiptoes to see if their new baby was there somewhere, and then he froze. Becca was at the front of the line with her older sister. Mitch slowly lowered himself to his normal height and stepped back, allowing his parents to block his view. He hoped it would make it impossible for Becca to see him.

As the line moved forward, Mitch continued to adjust where he was standing. He did not want Becca to spot him. There was no way she wouldn't say something nasty, and then he'd have to explain some things to his parents. Things he didn't want them to know. He could hear her whine "that took *forever*" and thought he was almost safe. He could tell by where her voice came from that they were walking toward the door. He glanced up just as Becca and her sister were passing him, and to his horror he and Becca locked eyes.

Becca stopped walking, eyes narrowed, and looked like she was about to unleash a string of curse words at Mitch when her sister ran into the back of her. "God, Becca, get out of the way!" She shoved Becca, and Mitch was forced to grab her arm to steady her.

Becca, barely catching her cup of ice cream stumbled and as she straightened, Mitch could see the humiliated look on her face. Mitch felt sorry for her and started to say something to make her feel better, but Becca's sister beat him to it.

"Come on, you idiot. I don't have all day!" The taller version of Becca stood at the door with one hand on her hip and the other holding her ice cream cone.

"Don't touch me," Becca hissed in Mitch's ear as she pulled her arm from his grip. She hurriedly walked to the door, and they were gone.

Mitch felt a combination of great relief and pity. He wasn't always fond of Addie, but he'd never treat her like that, especially not in public in front of fifteen strangers. But he was sure glad Becca didn't say anything horrible to him in front of his family.

Mom put her hand on his back. "What was that about?" she asked, nudging him forward in line.

Mitch shook his head, shrugged, and turned his attention to the chalkboards on the wall that listed the day's ice cream flavors. He stared up at them, looking at the words but unable to read them. That had been a close call. A *very* close call.

17

GINNY

Ginny burrowed under her covers as her room filled with the morning sunlight. She was comfortable, plus Lucky had snuck in sometime during the night and was taking up more than half of her bed. She wouldn't be able to get out without disrupting his sleep, so she stayed curled up next to him.

She felt happy. Her dad was downstairs, probably making something amazing for breakfast, she'd spent most of the weekend with her friends, who she'd see again in a couple of hours, and she'd spent time with Mitch yesterday. Several hours with him *in person*. She smiled broadly and stretched her legs, pointing her toes.

There was light knocking at her door and Dad peeked in. "Rosco? Are you awake?" She sat up, partially, not able to sit up all the way with Lucky next to her.

Dad came in holding two steaming mugs. He sat down on the end of her bed, nudging Lucky's legs with his knee to make room, and handed Ginny a cup of hot cocoa. Lucky sighed heavily and fell right back to sleep.

"What do we have for homework? Let's plot out our day," he said, sipping from his mug of coffee.

Ginny, who lost some of her covers when she tried to sit up, pressed her hands into the hot mug to warm herself. "I have math, health, and English. Math and health won't take that long, but I have a lot of reading."

"Okay, let's eat breakfast, you can do an hour of homework, then we can get ready for the movie. When we get back, you will need to finish your homework before we do anything else. Deal?"

"Deal," agreed Ginny.

He stood up and walked to her door. "Breakfast in five. Lucky, let's go outside." He patted his thigh a few times and Lucky jumped down from Ginny's bed and trotted past Dad into the hallway.

Ginny sat in the warmth of her bed, with her hot chocolate, and realized that *this* is what she missed. When Dad was around, it was like they were a unit. She felt like she was part of something. When it was just her and Mom it was as if they were roommates who ate meals together sometimes, but it never felt like they were a *family*. Her mom just wasn't warm and open like Dad was, at least not for the past year. Probably because she was raised by Grandma Weber, who was about as warm as a flagpole in winter.

Ginny heard a chirp from her computer and reluctantly left her toasty bed. She bent over her desk and smiled.

Sportstatsguy: Hey you!

Ginny sat down and set her mug next to her laptop.

Rosco: Hey you!

She almost asked how yard work had gone yesterday, but she couldn't remember if Sportstatsguy ever told her he was doing that yesterday. Her smile faltered. This was getting confusing.

Sportstatsguy: How is having your dad home?
Rosco: Soooo good. I think I only have him for a few more days. :(
Sportstatsguy: Maybe he can come home more often?
Rosco: Hopefully. What are you doing today?
Sportstatsguy: I might get roped into taking Addie to a movie.
But I had an idea.

Ginny paused. A movie? What if they went to the same one? There were three theaters in town, so it wasn't likely they'd run into each other. But still. She was going to have to be careful about what she said.

Rosco: What?
Sportstatsguy: My school has a social media site called KenChat.
I don't have a profile on it but I was thinking I should get
one and advertise Sports with Mitch. *Right?*

Ginny sat up. This was a great idea! She was annoyed she hadn't thought of it herself. Mitch wasn't on KenChat because he was new. And a boy. Some guys never made profiles, but this would help him get more listeners.

Rosco: TOTALLY.
Sportstatsguy: Yeah? Okay, I'll do that today. Talk later?
Rosco: Yes! Can't wait!

She shut her laptop and got dressed. This could change every-thing for Mitch. If he got enough listeners, he could quit with the secrets and just go back to sports. There were enough kids in the middle and high schools that cared about sports. He'd be able to keep his podcast and not worry about how to keep getting more people.

■ ■ ■

Ginny stood in front of the candy selection with her hands on her hips. She loved Whoppers, and Milk Duds, and M&Ms. And really buttery movie popcorn. She couldn't decide. She'd had pancakes, eggs, and bacon just two hours ago, yet her stomach growled as she weighed her sweet options.

Dad cleared his throat and she looked up. "So?" he asked. He was standing at the counter with his wallet open.

Ginny returned her gaze to the candy. "I can't decide."

"Well, the movie will be half over if you don't pick some-thing soon."

"How 'bout this?" Robin came over to her. "We can split my popcorn and then I'll get one candy and you get another, and we'll split those too."

Ginny nodded decisively and grabbed Milk Duds and Whoppers and set them on the glass countertop. She smiled at the high school boy who stood at the cash register. He looked bored and kept snapping his gum. Dad paid and they moved over so the people behind them could order while they waited for their soda and popcorn.

"Okay, ladies, Alicia's mom will be parked out front when the movie is over and she'll drive you all home. Have fun!" He kissed Ginny's forehead and headed for the door.

The girls buttered their popcorn and, with arms full of treats, walked to theater seven. They were seeing a new movie about a talking dog. It was a little young for them, but they loved dog movies and didn't care that it was just PG.

They sat in a row that had a railing in front of it that they could put their feet on. As they settled into their seats, Emily look back at the rows behind them. "It's packed," she whispered. "And we're like the oldest kids here!"

Robin turned around and quickly turned forward again. "Mitch is here!" she whispered loudly.

They all looked back and Ginny's stomach sank. Mitch was there, sitting next to his little sister Addie. She sat next to another younger girl who was grabbing a handful of popcorn from a bag that Sam Rasmussen held. Ginny jerked back toward the front.

"Is he with Sam? *Again*?" Alicia asked.

Ginny could feel Robin looking at her. She was still the only one who knew Ginny liked Mitch. "Well, their sisters are friends, so it's probably not like they're out on a date or something," Robin offered, handing Ginny the box of Whoppers to open.

Ginny took the box and ripped open the top. She poured a handful of Whoppers into her palm and handed it back to

Robin. How could they be at the exact same theater seeing the exact same movie? She should have insisted they see something that was PG-13 so there wasn't a chance they'd run into Mitch and his sister. And Sam. She blew out a gust of air.

"I don't know," said Emily, looking back again. "She's flirting a *lot*."

Ginny felt like her head might explode. She didn't know what to say or do. She needed time to think. She took a long drink of her Cherry Coke and was grateful the lights were finally going down for the movie. She'd have two hours to decide what to do next.

Robin leaned over to take the cup she was sharing with Ginny. "We will figure this out," she whispered so quietly Ginny almost didn't hear her.

Ginny looked at her and they nodded silently. She had to believe Robin was right. She *had* to.

Ginny was in the large theater bathroom looking in the mirror. She tightened her ponytail and pulled her T-shirt so the bottom stuck out just below her cheerleading jacket. In the first half of the movie, one of the talking dogs had said something that made Ginny feel better. He was talking to his owner, a boy named Ethan, and he said, "Sometimes you have to do things that are scary but it's the only way to go after your dreams. Nobody's dreams come true by hiding and doing nothing." It was true and Ginny knew it. If she wanted Mitch to like her, she'd have to tell him who she was. And she'd have to do it soon. Because Sam Rasmussen wasn't wasting any time.

She was putting on lip gloss when she heard the door open and Addie Henry walked through the door. Ginny felt like she knew Addie because she'd been hearing about her from Sportstatsguy since they "met" online. She almost said hi, but didn't when she realized Addie didn't know *her* and walked right past her to the row of stalls. Ginny put the gloss back into her bag and walked out the door. She took two steps and stopped. Mitch was sitting on a bench in the empty theater lobby.

"Ginny, hey," he said, standing up. "I saw you guys come in after we did. The dog movie?"

Ginny blushed. She was a little embarrassed to be seeing that movie. Maybe they should have seen the new romantic shark attack movie. "Yep. You've gotta love talking dogs, right?" Was that cologne she smelled? He smelled so good.

Mitch laughed, but nervously. Why would he be nervous around *her*, she wondered. "Yeah, I'm here with my sister and her friend," he said. After a pause he added, "and her older sister is Sam, the girl you met on Friday."

Did he not want to admit he was with Sam? That's what it seemed like. "She seems nice," Ginny offered.

"Oh, yeah, she is. Our sisters have been friends forever, so it's kind of like we're cousins or something. Or . . ." he trailed off. He was obviously trying to emphasize that this was not a date.

"Right, I know what you mean," Ginny said, shyly. "I have to get back in there or Robin will eat all of our candy."

Mitch looked relieved. "Okay, see you later," he said and he sat back down on the bench Ginny had found him on.

Ginny smiled and walked back to the theater. When she was sitting next to Robin she leaned toward her. "He is definitely not on a *date*," she whispered. Robin looked at her wide-eyed. "I just ran into him in the lobby. He said she's like a *cousin*." She smiled broadly and Robin smiled back. Ginny knew she still had to do something and do it soon, but maybe Sam wasn't as big of a threat as she thought. She snuck a peek at the spot where they were sitting and saw Mitch and Addie returning to their seats. Sam smiled at Mitch, and Ginny's unease returned. She was so pretty and, irritatingly, she was nice too. Ginny turned back to the screen and wondered if Mitch was being honest when he played down their relationship. Her temporary feelings of triumph quickly faded and she was soon back to plotting how she'd get Mitch to like *her*.

18

MITCH

Playing the baritone sax was cool, but even for Mitch, who was 5'10" already, it was gigantic. The case came up to his chest and it was really heavy. Mr. Swan had arranged for him to have a sax that he used at school and one that stayed at home so he didn't have to carry it back and forth, but even getting it to different parts of the house was a challenge.

He was trying to get to the basement so his practicing wouldn't bug everyone else, but he had to take it one step at a time, the case thudding each time he went down.

"Mitchel! Be *careful,* for crying out loud," his mom yelled from her office upstairs. "I doubt you want your lawn money going toward a new sax!"

Mitch tried to quiet the thuds and awkwardly made it to the basement. Thankfully, the case had wheels, and even on the carpeted floor he was able to roll it to the family room.

His weekend had been so full that he hadn't touched his homework or his sax. He had five hours until his show and tons to do, but he didn't even care. This was the best weekend he'd had in as long as he could remember.

Mitch assembled the brass instrument, one piece at a time, and then set up his music stand. He was still getting used to the new sax. The keys were more spread out so his fingers had to reach a lot further, and he also had to blow harder because the air had further to go. He knew that practicing more often would help a lot, but there were always other things to do. He blew a couple of notes and got out the sheet music Mr. Swan wanted him working on. On Friday, he was invited to play another concert with the high school musicians in October. Mitch couldn't believe Mr. Swan thought he was ready for that, and he knew he couldn't let him down.

He started with songs he knew by heart. It was a little different with the bari, but he was using them to get a better feel for the instrument. As he played his mind wandered. His world today was a completely different place than it had been two weeks ago. How could things change so quickly?

The best part was Josh, Tyler, Jin, and Zach. They'd fallen back into a cohesive group. Everyone got along, there wasn't any drama, and they were all good kids. None of his old friends had changed so drastically that Mitch didn't still really like them. Friday night had been fun and easy.

"I think you know 'Hot Cross Buns' well enough," Addie interrupted his thoughts. "Don't you know any other songs?"

"Don't you have something to do?" Mitch asked, annoyed.

"Umm, yeah, that's why I'm down here. I have to fold clothes, and in case you didn't notice, the laundry room is in the basement." She turned and walked to the laundry room before Mitch could respond.

He slipped the sheet music for 'Hot Cross Buns' to the back of his pile and shuffled the pages until he found one with basic note exercises.

The weirdest part of the weekend was the girls. He hadn't thought about girls this much, *ever*. Admittedly, he'd only really spent time with Rosco until this year. And that was all online. Now there seemed to be girls cycling through his mind on a regular rotation. There was Sam, who he was now convinced did in fact like him. Rosco, of course, his best friend *and* a girl. And there was Ginny. Something about Ginny drew him to her. A familiarity he couldn't put his finger on. He stopped playing and stared at the notes. Should he be thinking about asking someone to Homecoming?

His mom walked into the family room holding an overflowing basket of clean clothes. "You have fifteen more minutes, and I think you need to move onto the harder stuff. Don't you need to practice for the next concert?"

Mitch nodded and found the music for one of the new songs.

"I'll call down when you're done," Mom said over her shoulder as she walked away.

He let go the thoughts of girls, and Homecoming, and slowly and choppily started playing.

■ ■ ■

Mitch may not have looked at www.yourwholetruth.com since Friday, but apparently plenty of other people did. It was up to 423 secrets. Mitch shook his head in disbelief. At least he didn't have to worry about the fact that he'd only watched one game all weekend. He was too busy doing stuff. His entire podcast could be about secrets. He guessed most of his listeners wouldn't even mind if he didn't talk sports. This wasn't something he loved. Sports was the reason for the podcast in the first place. It's what he actually cared about when he thought about how important *Sports with Mitch* really was to him. It was disappointing that many of his new listeners probably didn't want him to talk about sports at all. He sighed heavily with the realization that the new listeners were the only thing that could save the show.

Mitch finished his practicing, homework, chores, and dinner with his family with just forty-five minutes left before his show. He needed to pick tonight's secrets and check ESPN for sports news. He could talk about the high school game that he'd attended on Friday and the parts of the college game he'd watched with Dad. That could take up some time if people called in.

He decided on four secrets. He'd have to fake his way through the sports, which, if he was honest with himself, made him feel a little sick. He flipped the "On Air" sign and shut his door. At the press of a button, the University of Minnesota rouser played.

"Hey, you've found *Sports with Mitch*, Sunday edition. Tonight we have more secrets and we have to talk about Friday's game. Kenwood continued their winning streak thanks to Julius Crawford and his amazing field goal. The rest of the game needs some breaking down. I'm hoping there are some Kenwood Royals that can weigh in tonight an—" Mitch glanced at the number of listeners that were currently tuned in and stopped mid-sentence. There were 278 listeners. He hit refresh, thinking there must be a mistake, and the number jumped to 292.

"Sorry about that, where was I? The game. I hope some of you players will call in so we can talk about our defense. Let's start with a secret first. Here you go!" Mitch pressed play and a computerized girl's voice started talking.

"I am in ninth grade and I have a job. I'm not old enough to actually have a job, but we have a family friend that has a business. I work at the cash register. Last week I took ninety dollars. My mom can't keep a job for more than a couple of weeks at a time and we never have enough money. I was so tired of making me and my brother ramen noodles every night for dinner, I just wanted to take us to McDonald's so we could get out of the apartment and eat a big dinner. They didn't even notice the money was gone, and I feel really bad, but now I keep thinking about taking more. I'm worried we're going to get kicked out of our apartment. I don't know. I just had to tell someone."

Mitch clicked his mouse and coughed to get rid of the lump in his throat. This one made him really sad, but many of the secrets he was getting *were* sad. He couldn't only play benign secrets or people would stop listening. He chose them carefully because he wanted to air problems people could relate to. Thankfully he had two calls right away. "You're on *Sports with Mitch*, what do you have to say about this last secret?"

"Hi, Mitch. She can't keep stealing. She's going to get caught and get fired. She has to come clean and tell her boss what is going on. Then she needs to find a way to repay it."

Mitch wasn't sure that was the right answer. "Thanks. Next caller, what do you think?"

The caller started talking but too quietly to hear.

"I'm sorry, can you speak up?"

"Sorry." The voice was deep. It made Mitch think of the linebackers on the Kenwood team. He pictured a big burly guy. "Yeah, so this happened to me. I had to take care of my two little sisters because my dad can't hold a job. But I called a place called Rise Up and they helped me. I think they will be able to help you too. Call them before you try to steal again. I don't think that's going to help, and you don't want to make things worse."

Mitch agreed. "Thanks, caller. Let's do one more before we move onto football. This goes out to my buddy Jin." He pressed play and another girl started talking.

"So, I know the other day there was a girl who said she likes Jin Zhao. I really don't want to be mean, but I like him too. And we're friends. I want to ask him to the Homecoming dance but I also don't want to be mean to the first girl who told her secret. I don't know what to do."

Mitch couldn't keep a straight face. Jin was going to be a maniac in school tomorrow. Again, he had callers right away. "You're on *Sports with Mitch*, what do you think our confessor should do?"

"It's my humble opinion," Jin started, "that this person should just ask Jin to the dance."

Mitch laughed out loud. "Is this the famous Jin Zhao himself?"

"It is, Mitch, and let me just say, you have excellent taste in secrets."

"Yeah, you're welcome. Let's talk sports."

Mitch rehashed the good and bad parts of Friday's football game, and thankfully got a couple of callers that analyzed the plays and talked about upcoming opponents. He talked briefly about the college game he'd seen and some of the games he'd read about on ESPN, just highlights. Then he had only enough time to play the last two secrets and take some calls. He played the first one.

"I'm a guy and I'm in eighth grade. Nobody knows this but I like to wear makeup. I spend hours at home watching YouTube tutorials and figuring out different looks. My parents know, and they are cool with it, but I'm too scared to tell anyone else. I know they will make fun of me or tell me I'm gay. I'd love to do more than just hide in my room and play with makeup but I don't know how without making my life miserable."

At first there were no callers. Mitch turned on his mic and said, "What do you think, listeners? Does anyone have any ideas?" Suddenly he had four calls coming in.

"Hey! I do plays at the Kenwood Community Theater and they are always looking for people to help with makeup for our productions. This guy might be perfect! The website is kenwooddrama.org. Find the number there and call and ask for Gary. I'm sure he can hook you up!"

Mitch clicked on the next caller.

"I don't know if this guy lives in Kenwood or not, but my mom owns a salon in town and she'd totally let him come in and watch the makeup sessions and maybe work on kids or middle schoolers once he's good enough. Tell him to call or email Jackie at Fusion Salon and Spa on Main Street. It's across from Book Nook."

Mitch glanced at the time and realized he was about out of it. "I hate to say it, but we're out of time. I can take one more caller."

"Hey, Mitch, I have a question for ya," said a male caller.

Mitch smiled. He was loving that he had callers and the banter they shared. "What's that?"

"I'm just wondering, are you going to stop talking about sports? Because the name of your show would indicate it has a sports focus but tonight it sounds more like a teen advice hotline. You didn't even go into baseball playoffs or college football. Do I need to find a new sports podcast to listen to?"

Mitch swallowed and his cheeks reddened. He didn't want to admit it, but the caller was right. Mitch was getting so caught up in the secrets, and the extra listeners they brought to his show, that he'd totally dropped the ball on sports. It had been at the back of his mind the whole time, and he'd even felt a little sick about it at times, but he pushed it all aside with the idea that new listeners were the most important part. Sports was literally the whole point of the podcast in the first place. He didn't know what to say. Finally, unsure if his voice would even work properly, he said, "No need for a new podcast. There will be more sports on Tuesday, I promise. That's it for—" Mitch paused, embarrassed. "That's it for *Sports with Mitch*. Tune in Tuesday."

Shutting his laptop, Mitch got up from his desk and went to the window that faced the fields. He wasn't sure what to do. He couldn't only talk about sports or he'd lose his new listeners, which he desperately needed. He couldn't only expose secrets or he'd lose the listeners he'd had the whole time. Not to mention, he was listed on Podder as a "sports podcast." He turned and flopped face first onto his bed, discouraged. None of this felt right, or even good. His excitement over new listeners now felt childish and short-sighted. He didn't want to be a gossip show host.

He wanted to talk to Rosco. She always had good ideas. He reached for his laptop when the text alert went off on his phone.

Sam Rasmussen - 8:17pm: You can't win! What ru gonna do?

19

GINNY

Ginny looked at her reflection in the mirror in the girls' locker room and tugged at the bottom of her cheerleading skirt. The bus for the girls' soccer game left in ten minutes, and all Ginny really wanted to do was talk to Mitch. She saw him for a second before first period, but he left before lunch for doctors' appointments. She hadn't talked to him since last night's show and she knew he must be reeling from that last call. She felt her phone vibrate and pulled it out to see that Dad was calling.

"Hello?"

"Rosco, it's Dad. I have to go back to Chicago earlier than I planned. I'm grabbing a flight tonight."

Ginny's stomach dropped. "But," she stammered, "why?"

"Something came up at work. But listen, your mom will be home tomorrow and Grandma Weber will pick you up when you get home from the game at five, okay?"

Ginny's throat tightened and she squeezed her eyes shut.

Dad continued, "I'll be back before you know it, I promise."

She could only muster a whisper. "Okay. Love you."

"Love you too, Rosco. Cheer your heart out tonight! And don't forget to grab the mail when you get home."

This was too much. Just when she'd gotten used to having Dad around again, to feeling like home was *home* again, he was leaving.

"Gin? Bus is leaving!" a voice called from the locker room entrance. Ginny threw her phone into her cheer bag and wiped at her damp eyes. She hustled through the locker room and into the school lobby, where the squad was waiting. She nodded, and they followed her out the front doors to the bus that waited outside.

As she climbed the stairs, she saw Emily sitting a few seats back, her curly red hair pulled up into a bun and held back with a blue headband that matched her soccer jersey. Emily waved and Ginny slid into the seat next to her.

Emily's smile turned to a look of concern. "What? What is it?" she asked.

Ginny shook her head, doubting her ability to talk about it without starting to cry. "I'll tell you later," she croaked.

Before Emily could respond, the girls' soccer coach started talking about game strategy. Ginny closed her eyes and leaned her head back on the green vinyl seat. She pretended to sleep for the entire ride to Lakeland Middle School, and when the bus stopped again, she was up and out of her seat before Emily had the chance to ask her anything else.

Cheering middle school soccer, girls' or boys', was not Ginny's favorite. It wasn't that she didn't like soccer—she did. And it was fun cheering for Emily. But there was usually a very small crowd. Only some parents could make it, since the games were played right after school and most adults were still at work. There was never a big group of kids at them either. Cheering to a small crowd was a lot of work. It was so much more fun when there were tons of people to cheer with them. Without an audience, the games seemed to last forever.

The squad stood in a line facing the field, their hands holding their pom-poms behind their backs. "Hey, Gin, can we try some stunts since there's, like, nobody here?" asked Ashrita, who had stepped forward from the line so she could see Ginny.

Grateful for the distraction, Ginny nodded. "Let's try the Be Aggressive basket toss. Ashrita, do you want to go up first?"

"Yes!" Ashrita responded, bouncing with excitement.

Ginny directed the girls to the correct formation and ran through the cheer a couple of times before they tried it.

Together they yelled "BE AGGRESSIVE" and they clapped twice. Then, as they spelled it out, they stepped into a circle and lowered their hands in the middle. Ashrita stepped in and they tossed her into the air when they next said "BE AGGRESSIVE." She landed back into their arms as they said "GOT TO BE AGGRESSIVE." Once she was deposited back to the ground, the girls clapped.

"You guys, that was *awesome*!" Ginny gushed. "Let's do it again, who wants to try this time?" Four hands went into the air and they all laughed. "Okay, Holly, you're up!"

They spent the rest of the game tossing each other into the air and trying different stunts while flying. Spread eagle, pike, and summersaults. Ginny couldn't believe the progress they were making as a middle school cheer squad. When the final whistle blew she was surprised to feel disappointed the game was over so soon. The girls packed up their stuff and before heading back to the bus, Ginny glanced at the scoreboard. The Royals won 3-2.

■ ■ ■

By the time Ginny climbed into Grandma's big mint-green sedan, her mood had improved significantly. Mitch, and her dad, weren't the only things Ginny had going for her. She had her cheerleading squad. If they continued to practice their stunts, they might be able to compete next summer. That would be amazing.

"Hey, Grandma," Ginny said.

Grandma sighed, and straightened in her seat. "Hay is for horses. You can do better than that."

Ginny smirked. She wasn't going to let Grandma get to her today. She wanted to get home to find new stunts on YouTube that she could try at practice this week.

Grandma turned the opposite direction of Ginny's house. "Where are we going?" Ginny asked, confused.

Another heavy sigh. "As usual, your father didn't give me much notice about staying with you tonight and I already had plans. My bridge game starts in ten minutes. You'll have to just . . ." she trailed off, concentrating on the next turn she was making. "You can do homework until I'm done."

Ginny sat up straighter. A couple of Grandma's girlfriends lived in apartments on Main Street by Book Nook and The Drip. "Where are you playing?"

"The party room at Myrna's."

Ginny smiled. She loved Myrna, but even better, she lived in the Main Street Senior Co-op. "Can I do homework at The Drip while you're playing cards?"

Grandma shook her head ever so slightly. "You know, business owners don't like it when kids loiter."

Ginny thought she knew what "loiter" meant, but she wasn't sure. "I have money," she started, hoping that was the right response. "So I'll buy something there."

"You'll have to walk from Myrna's. I don't have time to drop you off," Grandma said as she drove right past The Drip.

Ginny watched it go by. "That's fine," she said. She missed Dad already.

The bell jingled when Ginny opened the door to The Drip. She set her backpack on a chair by a corner table and unzipped the front pocket, pulling out a ten dollar bill.

"On your own today?" Rachel asked, coming up front from the back office. She washed her hands in a little sink and then faced Ginny again.

"Yep!" Ginny looked at her options under the glass. "Can I have a chocolate milk, a turkey sandwich, and a cup of chocolate chocolate chip ice cream?"

Rachel pulled out the pre-wrapped turkey sandwich and set it in front of Ginny, then turned to make the chocolate milk. "Did your dad leave already?"

Ginny looked down. She didn't want to think about her dad being gone. She wanted to research cheerleading stunts. "He had to go back for work. My mom comes home tomorrow."

Rachel set the glass of chocolate milk down on the counter and pressed buttons on the iPad that was connected to the cash register. "Nine dollars even. Do you want to wait to have the ice cream until you're done with your sandwich?"

"Yes please, thanks." Ginny headed to her table with her sandwich and milk. As she opened her laptop and waited for it to wake up, she looked out the window. Outside she saw parents and kids up and down the street. She didn't see any other middle schoolers walking around alone. Loneliness settled over her like a fog.

As soon as her home screen appeared Ginny opened Chatter.

> *Rosco: Hey you. We haven't talked since your show!*
> *Sportstatsguy: I know! I have to run to some of my lawns quick.*
>   *Talk later? Need advice.*
> *Rosco: Yep! I'll be around.*

Ginny closed Chatter and stared at her screen. Her phone buzzed from her backpack and she pulled it out.

> *Robin Blair - 5:06pm: What r u doing? Wanna study English?*
> *Ginny Ross - 5:06pm: YES! But I'm at The Drip. With*
>   *grandma tonight and she's playing cards for a couple of*
>   *hours. Can you come here?*

Ginny unwrapped her sandwich and took a bite. Mustard squirted out the side and a large drop landed on her cheerleading skirt. She took some napkins and rubbed at it, only managing to make the spot bigger.

Robin Blair - 5:09pm: I can be there in fifteen minutes. Can your grandma drive me home?

Ginny thought about that. She could think up an excuse to make that happen.

Ginny Ross - 5:10pm: We can figure it out. See you soon!

Ginny took another bite of her sandwich. By the time Robin arrived she had gone through three napkins.

"Just in time for ice cream!" Ginny said standing up to throw her trash away.

Robin dropped her bag on the chair opposite where Ginny had been sitting. "Perfect timing!"

■ ■ ■

After inhaling their ice cream and studying English for forty-five minutes, Ginny and Robin got drinks to go and decided to walk up and down Main Street until it was time to meet Grandma.

Robin stopped in front of the window of a stationery and card shop. "What are you going to do about Mitch?" she asked as she peered in the glass at the displays of journals and pretty notecards.

Ginny took in a deep breath of the crisp fall air. It was chilly but not too cold, and it smelled like bonfires. She blew out and shook her head. "I don't know." She started walking to the next store, Robin trailing behind her.

"I was kind of hoping you'd say that," Robin said, catching up to Ginny. "I have an idea."

They stopped at the large window of a shoe store called Steppin' Out and looked in. They always had beautiful shoes that Ginny and Robin loved to look at and sometimes try on. It was almost empty, and Ginny looked at her watch. "We can look for fifteen minutes," she said, looking at Robin.

Robin nodded, and they pushed open the front door. The smell of shoe polish and new leather hit them as they walked in.

"Hi, girls," said a tall woman with crazy blonde curly hair. She had glasses stuffed into the pile of curls on top of her head. "Everything is 20 percent off, and I can hold shoes for twenty-four hours if you need to bring your parents back."

They smiled at her and started going down the aisles, slowly taking in all of the beautiful shoes that were surely too expensive for any kid to actually buy. Ginny nudged Robin. "What is your idea?" she asked quietly.

Robin turned and smiled. "Why don't you leave a secret on his website? I checked it out last night and you can put a title on your secret. You could title it something like 'a secret for Mitch' and tell him who you are." Her eyes were sparkling with excitement.

Ginny picked up bright-blue satin high heels that had jewels covering the pointed toe. "I don't know," she said as she ran her fingers over the white and blue stones. "What would I even say?" She returned the shoe to its small shelf on the wall.

"Mitch, this is Ginny Ross," Robin said in a fake voice. "I am also your good friend online and we should go to Homecoming."

Ginny guffawed. "Yeah, that would totally work."

Robin grinned. "You'd think of something, but he would find out the truth in your words, and he'd be alone so he would have time to think about it."

Ginny stepped through a beaded door opening to get to the back clearance room. The shelves that lined the three walls were full of summer sandals and strappy heels.

"The season closeouts back there are an extra 30 percent off," called the woman from the front of the store.

Robin was right. Telling Mitch the truth on his website might be the easiest way for Ginny to tell him. She'd get to tell him everything she wanted him to know without worrying about him stopping her or getting angry.

The buzzing of her phone interrupted her thoughts. She pulled it out of her jacket pocket to see a text from Grandma.

Grandma - 7:25pm: ???????

Ginny looked at it in confusion. She was supposed to meet grandma at 7:45. Her phone buzzed again.

Grandma - 7:26pm: Please get back here. We need to go.

Ginny frowned. Grandma must not have done well in her bridge game. She was competitive. She'd probably spend the entire car ride home complaining about her friends, women she'd known since Ginny's mom was a little girl.

It was either that or her back was really hurting her. She had changed her position several times on the drive over tonight. Maybe that was it.

Ginny typed a response and quickly stuffed the phone back in her pocket to avoid seeing Grandma's response.

Ginny - 7:26pm: Be right there. We have to drop Robin off, she can't find a ride.

20

MITCH

It wasn't like Mitch to forget things, especially when it came to his lawn business. He pulled up next to a blue mailbox and then reached for his stack of invoices. Normally Mitch delivered invoices on Sundays, but with everything that had happened over the weekend, he'd forgotten.

Mitch sifted through the envelopes, found the right one, and stuffed it in the mailbox on top of the mail that had already been delivered that day. Returning the invoices to the compartment he kept them in, Mitch started toward the houses on the other side of the junior high school.

As he drove he added the invoice totals in his head. He had four leaf services scheduled for next weekend and he had six lawns to mow before Sunday. It never seemed like too much when Mitch didn't have friends to hang out with, or concerts to practice for, or girls liking him, but now he wondered how he'd get it all done. Maybe Mom wouldn't notice if he failed a couple of his classes? He smirked at the thought.

Sports with Mitch had enough listeners to keep it going on Podder. For now. What Mitch couldn't figure out was how to hold on to those listeners. He couldn't just talk about people's secrets. The show was called *Sports with Mitch* for a reason. But when he talked about only sports he didn't get enough people to listen. When he didn't cover enough sports he got complaints from the people he actually *wanted* to be hearing and calling in to his show. It's not like he started a podcast with dreams of becoming a gossip reporter, which is what it was starting to feel like.

Rosco would have good advice. She always did.

Mitch turned onto Virginia Avenue. The Rosses lived halfway down the road on the right. It was a pretty street. Tall trees shaded the road and orange and red leaves covered the asphalt. It was windy, and leaves flew up from the street in swirls. He pulled up to Ginny's copper mailbox and opened it. He reached for his invoices when a gust of wind pulled some of the envelopes out of the mailbox and onto the street.

"Dang it!" Mitch climbed off of his lawn mower. The pieces of mail that fell out of the box were being blown with the leaves on the street. He scrambled to catch them all. Advertisements for house cleaning, mail from an airline, and several business-looking envelopes. He'd missed one piece that continued to be whisked further and further away. He chased it down and grabbed it by the corner. He breathed a sigh of relief and walked back to the mailbox, organizing the envelopes and postcards so it didn't look like he'd ravaged the Rosses' mail. As he did, he turned over the last one he'd picked up and froze. This wasn't a normal piece of mail.

Written in sharpie in large black letters on the front was the word ROSCO.

Mitch looked at the house. It looked like nobody was home. He added his invoice to the stack of mail and placed it back in the box, carefully, as if it might explode with mishandling. He got back on his mower and stared ahead. He couldn't make sense of this. After sitting for a couple of minutes, he started the mower and drove ahead. Things started to fall into place, little by little. Rosco's dad was back, and he'd seen Ginny's dad on Saturday. Ginny's last name is Ross. Could Ginny possibly be Rosco? Could Rosco be Ginny?

After leaving an invoice for the Stegoras, Mitch started his trip back home. His mind was spinning. He was thinking back to all of the times he'd talked to Rosco about school, or where she lived. How could he not have figured this out? He didn't even know what he felt about this. He felt stupid, and angry. Why hadn't Rosco/Ginny just told him who she was? She *had* to know who he was. Right? But he was also a little excited. Rosco was *Ginny*. He'd been thinking about Ginny a lot lately. Now he realized he probably knew her better than most people did.

Mitch felt overwhelmed with all of the things on his plate before this. Now he felt flabbergasted. He wanted to go running, to clear his head. By the time he pulled into his driveway, his mind was a jumble of mixed-up thoughts. As he parked, Addie came out of the garage with two bags of recycling in her hands.

"You missed your girlfriend," she said, smirking.

Mitch didn't have time for this, but he also didn't know what she was talking about. "Which one?" he asked, passing her on his way into the house.

"Sam. She and Julia were out riding bikes."

Mitch heard the cans and glasses clinking as Addie dropped the bags to the bottom of the bin. He couldn't think about Sam now. He had too much to sort through in his head. He ran up to his bedroom to change into sweats and headed back outside, calling, "I'm going for a run" over his shoulder.

■ ■ ■

Running was sometimes the only way for Mitch to clear his head in the year and a half he was being home-schooled. He loved his mom, but spending every day with her sometimes made alone time necessary. At first he just walked around the neighborhood, headphones in his ears, playing loud music. When he got stronger he started jogging. Now he could run a few miles without having to stop to walk or catch his breath.

Instead of going the direction of Ginny's house, Mitch ran deeper into his neighborhood, behind the junior high. Rap music played loud in his ears, allowing him to forget everything and just focus on the words of the songs and his feet hitting the pavement. Every time he ran he knew he should do it more often. It felt good using his body again. Healing had taken so long that doing anything physically challenging was invigorating.

Mitch ran faster than his usual pace, trying to outrun the reality of what he'd just learned. After two miles he slowed his speed to a jog.

Mom found the online programming. The participants had been warned not to share their information with one another. It was *possible* that Ginny didn't know who he was. But he had a sinking feeling that she did know. Why wouldn't she tell him, though?

He looked up and saw the fields behind school ahead. He'd run around the edges and have three miles done by the time he got home. A whistle blew to his right and he looked over at the track. The junior high cross country team was running drills for Mr. Shields. He was one of the phys-ed teachers at school and, apparently, the track coach. Mitch stopped to watch runners jumping hurdles and practicing relay hand-offs.

The idea came like one of those rare rain showers that appear out of nowhere on a sunny day. His mom wouldn't let him play contact sports anymore, but what about cross country? She let him run in the streets of Kenwood, surely she couldn't come up with a reasonable objection to him running on a track.

The whistle blew again and Mitch noticed Mr. Shields was walking long strides in his direction. "Okay, let's finish with sprints, GO!" He blew the whistle one more time and then stopped in front of Mitch, his eyes still on his runners and gripping a clipboard in his hands. He was tall, probably 6'5", and he wore sweatpants and a Kenwood Track and Field T-shirt.

Mitch felt like he'd been caught spying. "Hi, Mr. Shields."

"I've seen you running around the fields over the past year. I didn't realize who you were until you came back to school."

Mitch shifted his weight, not sure how to ask the question that was burning in his mind. "It's the only thing my mom will really let me do. I mean, athletically. And I live right over there." He pointed across the fields to his house.

Mr. Shields nodded.

"So," Mitch started, nervously. "I'm guessing tryouts have already . . ."

Mr. Shields held up his hand, interrupting Mitch, and blew his whistle again. "Okay, that's it for today! See you tomorrow!" He yelled and then finally turned his full attention to Mitch. "Actually, I'd really like to add a few more people. It's a small group, and I need more talent. I've seen you sprint by here, you're fast. Would your parents let you join us?"

The shock caused Mitch's voice to temporarily stop working. "I think so," he croaked.

"Listen, why don't you give me their phone number and I'll give them a call tonight. We'll see what we can do." He turned to a blank page on his clipboard and wrote down the numbers Mitch gave him.

"Hopefully I'll see you here in the next couple of days!" He nodded at Mitch and started toward school.

Mitch was thunderstruck. Within an hour he had not only found out that Ginny Ross was Rosco, but he'd found a sport in which he might actually be able to participate. Something he'd been aching to do since the accident. He put his headphones back in his ears, pressed play, and took off in a sprint toward home. Grinning.

■ ■ ■

Mom looked skeptical. In the five minutes since she answered the phone, she'd said very little. Mitch could barely contain himself. He wanted to yell 'Put it on speaker!!!'" so he could hear what was being said. Now she started talking, explaining Mitch's injuries and the healing process. Then she was quiet again. Mitch leaned his head back and blew a gust of air out. He started counting the copper tiles that lined the ceiling of the kitchen.

Finally, Mom spoke again, and was wrapping up. "I appreciate the call and your insight. We'll talk about it tonight and get back to you tomorrow, will that work?" She nodded and said goodbye. She looked at Mitch with an expression he couldn't read. It was part sadness and part resignation, but he also saw hope in her face.

The door to the garage opened and Addie rushed past in her karate uniform. Dad came in behind her, setting his briefcase on one of the chairs tucked up against the kitchen table. He kissed Mom and went to the fridge to grab a soda, then sat across from Mitch at the table. He loosened his tie and then popped open the top of the can.

"So," he said, pausing to take a sip. "Sounds like we have a decision to make." Mr. Shields called Dad before he called Mom, so they both had the chance to ask questions and hear about the season.

Mitch sat up in his chair. He felt like someone on trial about to receive the verdict.

Mom set her glass of red wine down on the table, the glass making a light ting on the wood. "Mitchel, you have a lot of commitments right now. You have your lawn business, *Sports with Mitch*, this new group you've been invited to play sax with, and new friends that you are excited to spend time with again. All amazing things that you should be so proud of." She was rubbing her pointer finger around the rim of the wine glass as she spoke, but she was looking Mitch right in the eyes.

He couldn't tell where she was going with this. Would she say he had too much going on and couldn't join the team?

"But," she continued, "you've been wanting to play sports ever since the accident and this could actually work."

Mitch jumped out of his chair and ran around the table to hug Mom.

"Hold on! Hold on!" she said, laughing. "I'm not done!"

Mitch stood expectantly. There was a "but" coming.

"You simply can't do it all, honey. It's too much."

Mitch sat back down. He felt a little defeated, but mostly, his body just buzzed with the excitement of joining a real team again.

Dad spoke up now. "You will need to give one or two things up, buddy. You won't have time for it all, you won't have the energy, and we're not willing to let you wear yourself out *or* fall behind in school."

"Okay," Mitch said quickly. "Okay, I understand. I'll give something up."

Mom sipped her wine and set the glass back down. "Why don't you sleep on it and let's talk again in the morning."

Dad was smiling broadly at Mitch. He knew how badly Mitch had wanted to do something, to compete, over the years. "Coach Shields wants you at practice tomorrow but we'll need to get you running shoes and practice gear first. We can do that tomorrow night."

"He's checking in with you tomorrow at school. We will reconvene in the morning to make a plan." Mom was smiling now too. And it wasn't her sad/scared smile, the one she gave when she was nervous about him hurting himself again. She was actually happy for him.

Mitch felt his throat tighten. "Thank you," he choked. He went back to their side of the table and the three of them shared an awkward hug, his parents still sitting at the table and him bending down to reach them.

He started for the stairs; there was still reading to do for school and he had to tell Rosco. She would die when she heard. He stopped walking as he remembered what had come *before* he ran into Mr. Shields and his track team. Ginny Ross was Rosco. He shook his head, not willing to let the confusion and uncertainty spoil the high he felt, and he took the stairs two at a time as he imagined himself jumping hurdles at a track meet in front of a cheering crowd.

21

GINNY

What could she say?

Ginny splashed hot water on her face, rinsing the foamy white cleanser off, and then dabbed a towel to her wet cheeks and forehead.

She looked into the mirror and tried to come up with the words she needed to tell Mitch who she really was.

"Genevieve, what *are* you doing?" Grandma yelled up the stairs and Ginny cringed. She'd been particularly displeased about driving Robin home even though she only lived a couple of miles out of the way. Ginny put dots of white cream on places she was sure were destined to turn into pimples and tightened her robe as she walked out of the bathroom.

"I was washing my face, Grandma," she hollered down over the banister.

Ginny thought she heard a pill bottle rattling. Finally, Grandma called up, "You need to be in bed."

It was still a little early for bed, but she could see what Mitch was up to. Grandma wouldn't know the difference. "Okay, goodnight, Grandma. Love you."

She heard the TV being turned on downstairs. That would be the extent of their interaction tonight. Ginny was used to Grandma's less-than-warm personality, but it still made her feel bad from time to time. She knew it wasn't her that made Grandma crabby, she knew Grandma's back was probably hurting her. She sighed and went to her room. Lucky was sleeping on her bed, and Ginny's heart swelled. At least she had him. He loved her no matter what.

Ginny climbed into bed, trying not to disturb Lucky's sleep, and opened her laptop. Nothing from Mitch. "Hmm," she said out loud. Lucky stretched out at the sound of her voice, leaving her even less room than she'd had before. She wasn't sure what her next move should be. She could go to www.yourwholetruth.com and put her secret there, but what if Mitch never got to it? At the rate people were leaving messages for him, hers could sit there for days, maybe even weeks, before he heard it. She couldn't risk it. Homecoming was next weekend; she didn't have time to waste.

Opening a new document, Ginny tried to figure out where to start. She started to type quickly, not giving herself too much time to think about the words she was using. Her mind started to wander. She could print it and put it in Mitch's locker. Or on the website. Or—she stopped typing to let the thought settle. She could hack into his podcast one last time. Take over his show and tell him and all of his listeners that she,

Ginny Ross, was his long-time online friend and wanted him to go to Homecoming with her. Ginny tilted her head, thinking about the potential fallout.

She quickly opened a second new document and typed PROS & CONS at the top of the page.

PROS

1. Mitch would know the truth.
2. She'd get an answer about Homecoming.
3. Listeners might think it's romantic.

CONS

1. Mitch might be mad that she hacked the show.
2. Mitch would realize she didn't "fix" his hacker problem, she WAS the hacker problem.
3. He could get mad she never told him who she really was.
4. She'd lose him as an online friend *and* a real friend.

Ginny stared at the blue screen. Maybe it wasn't such a good idea after all. She clicked out of the list and went back to what she'd been writing as an explanation. Not knowing what to say, she set her laptop aside and curled around Lucky, who was snoring quietly. Ginny wanted real people around her. Not online friends, not a dad who lived 410 miles away, and not a mom who was in and out of their house all the time. With her eyelids starting to get heavy, she closed her laptop and set it on the floor next to her bed. Then she turned off her bedside light, knowing Grandma surely wouldn't come up to tuck her in.

■ ■ ■

Barking woke Ginny earlier than normal. Lucky jumped from her bed and down the stairs, alerting everyone that the garbage trucks were going down the street. Blurry-eyed, Ginny squinted at the clock. She wondered if Mitch would be online before school.

The thought got her up, and she headed for the shower. She got dressed in jeans and a hoodie from the university where Dad worked. After drying and straightening her hair, she sat down at her desk and opened Chatter.

Rosco: Morning!

She waited. Impatiently tapping her short fingernails on her desk. As seconds stretched into minutes, she got up to find shoes. She squatted in front of her closet and dug through shoes, slippers, and boots until she found a fuzzy pair to pull over the bottom of her jeans. Her laptop chirped and she leapt to her desk.

Sportstatsguy: I'm joining the track team!!!

Ginny's mouth dropped open. Mitch had been talking about wanting to play sports since she first met him. She couldn't believe his mom was finally letting him do something.

Rosco: Track?

Sportstatsguy: Yep! I ran by the fields yesterday and saw the team practicing. The coach asked if I wanted to join.

Ginny could picture Mr. Shields's running practice. She knew Mitch went running sometimes, but she'd never thought about him joining the track team. It was perfect for him. He'd get to compete again, and it wasn't a contact sport like football or hockey which she knew he wasn't allowed to play anymore.

Rosco: That is so awesome!!!

Sportstatsguy: G2G. Have to have a family meeting quick. See you later.

Ginny's eyes widened. She stared at his last sentence in disbelief. They *never* said that. They were online friends only so there was never a chance that they'd actually see each other later.

"What just happened?" she asked out loud.

She stood slowly, brows furrowed, and looked around her room like she'd landed in an alternate universe. She needed to brush her teeth and eat breakfast but found it hard to move from where she was.

"Ginny! Don't you need to *leave*?" Grandma snapped Ginny out of her temporary paralysis.

Grabbing her backpack, Ginny ran down the stairs and straight out the front door, forgetting her teeth, breakfast, and saying goodbye.

■ ■ ■

One thing Ginny didn't forget that morning was to grab the mail as she passed the mailbox outside her house. She'd forgotten to bring it in the day before when she got home from school. She stuffed it into her backpack without looking at it. When she was standing at her locker, she got her books and notebooks out and the mail came out with them, falling onto the tile floor.

Robin was walking up to their locker and picked up the envelopes that slid further away. "This one is for you," she said, handing an envelope to Ginny.

The envelope had the name ROSS on the top left-hand corner, with their address beneath it. Across the front, in large black letters, it said ROSCO in Dad's crisp handwriting.

Robin opened their second locker and was looking in the mirror, separating her curls. Without turning toward Ginny, she whispered, "So? Did you think of a way to tell Mitch?"

Ginny looked up from the still-unopened envelope. "Yes," she said definitively. The answer surprised her because she hadn't consciously made a decision. But she did know what she had to do.

Robin spun to face her. "And?" she asked, excited.

Putting the envelope inside the front cover of her social studies book, Ginny glanced at her own reflection and shut the locker *gingerly* to keep the chandelier from falling. "I either need to tell him in person or I will tell him on Chatter. I'm not going to submit it on his website. It feels too important and personal."

They started walking toward Advisory. It occurred to Ginny that *all* of the secrets that she'd heard, the ones she'd exposed and the ones who gave up their own, were important and personal. She felt her face flush and she looked down as they rounded the corner to Mitch's hall.

"You okay?" Robin asked, looking sideways at Ginny.

Ginny nodded and managed "Mmm hmm."

Robin started to slow as they got close to Mitch's locker, where Josh, Tyler, and Jin were joking around. Ginny didn't want to stop. She felt off this morning. She pulled the letter from her book and said quietly, "I'm going to go read this." She walked into the classroom and slid into her desk, trying to ignore whatever they were talking about in the hall.

The note was written on lined paper and folded in three. Ginny unfolded it and started reading. As she did, any feeling of being "off" she'd had before faded and was replaced with growing glee. She couldn't believe what she was reading. She looked up, her eyes brimming with happy tears, something she wasn't familiar with, and saw Robin coming down the aisle of desks.

"Oh my gosh," Robin said, concerned. "What is *wrong*?"

Ginny grinned, knowing she probably looked like a maniac. "Not one thing," she exclaimed, trying to keep her cool. Before she could tell Robin more, Mr. Pedersen started taking attendance.

She passed the piece of paper she'd been gripping behind her, and Robin took it. Within a minute, Robin made a muffled squeal, and gave Ginny's shoulders a quick squeeze.

Dad was coming home, for good. He'd been working on a deal for months, and the meetings he had while he was home solidified his plan. He was going to work for the University of

Minnesota and was starting a STEM school for middle and senior high school kids. College students studying to be teachers would be working with the younger kids, and the idea was that it would improve STEM education for all involved. He was moving back to Minneapolis to run the program and he wanted Ginny to be involved too.

Ginny was so glad Robin was in this class. Robin knew how much Ginny missed her dad, and it would have killed her not to be able to tell someone. But now that Robin knew, she really wanted to tell Mitch. The thought of waiting all day to do so felt like torture.

The scraping of desk feet on the tile floor surprised Ginny. She realized they were moving into their groups, and she stood to do the same. When she turned her desk to face Robin's, she saw that she was reading the letter from Dad again and looked perplexed.

"So," started Robin. "Does this mean you'll be leaving Kenwood schools?"

Ginny tilted her head to the right and thought about it. She took the letter back from Robin and skimmed it again, quickly. There weren't enough details to know the answer to that, but could that be a possibility? "I don't know," Ginny responded slowly.

22

MITCH

Mitch felt conflicted as he watched Mrs. Applegren furiously writing math equations on the board. About a couple of things. He had to decide what to give up in order to run track for Kenwood. He knew he was stretched too thin, but he loved the things he was involved in.

Deep down, he knew what he had to do. *Sports with Mitch* was something he started when he was no longer able to *play* sports but couldn't bring himself to give up on them. In the past week or so, it had turned into something completely different. Part of him liked the notoriety he now had, but he didn't start the podcast to be a gossip.

Running track was his way back in. Working out, competing, having teammates, it was what he craved all along. *Sports with Mitch* filled a void to a point, but it never filled it completely.

Even more confusing was the Ginny/Rosco fiasco. He'd thought of that when he was brushing his teeth this morning, and it made him chuckle. He smirked at his own humor. Seriously, though, how long had she known who he was? The whole time? And how could he have been stupid enough not to figure it out himself?

The person he most wanted to talk to about this was, in fact, Rosco. But she'd lied. That was what upset him and made it hard for him to reconcile. She'd been lying, maybe since the beginning when they first "met" online. Now she saw him at school every day and she was *still* keeping the truth from him. He didn't get it.

He returned his attention to what Mrs. Applegren was writing and quickly knew she was still going over equations he'd learned last year with Mom. Maybe Ginny didn't want to be friends with the real Mitch. Maybe she didn't like him in person or something. This hadn't occurred to him until now and he didn't like the theory. Ginny was always nice, she smiled and was funny and sarcastic when he was around. Then why? Why would she keep this from him?

"Mr. Henry, can you tell me what x is in this equation?" Mrs. Applegren was pointing to an equation and looking at him.

He sat up, calculated in his head, and said, "Negative eighteen?"

"Are you asking me or telling me?"

"Telling you."

She started erasing one side of the board. "That's right. Does everyone understand how he got that answer?"

The class mumbled an uncertain "yes" and she was on to the next example.

Mitch loved school, but one of his favorite parts of the day was lunch. Having friends to sit with and talk to was a lot more fun than he remembered it being when he was in elementary school.

He sat between Jin and Tyler and opened his milk carton. Tyler was telling them what the student council had planned for the Homecoming dance. Mitch listened as he dug into his orange chicken.

"Are any of you guys going to actually go? I was kind of hoping we could go as a group or something," Josh said.

Jin laughed. "I'm in if my mystery woman actually asks me."

Zach sat across from Mitch, next to Josh. "I'm going to ask someone tonight. I'll let you know."

They all stared at him, surprised. He was the quiet one of the group.

Jin broke the silence. "Who are you asking?"

Zach shook his head and smiled. "I'll tell you if they say yes."

Josh turned to Tyler. "You can ask someone from a different school, right?"

Tyler nodded, chewing the turkey sandwich his dad sent with him every day.

Josh looked at Mitch. "You should ask Sam. I bet she'd say yes."

"Genius!" Jin pounded his fists on the table. "She would say yes, she's totally got a crush on you."

Mitch knew they were right, and Sam was a cool girl, but he didn't like her the way he thought you were supposed to like someone you brought to a school dance. "No," he said, realizing how he felt about her as he spoke. "I don't like her like that."

"That's too bad," Jin said, dramatically. "Breaking hearts left and right, this guy."

They all laughed, and Mitch was grateful when Zach changed the subject to football. He looked down the lunch table and saw Ginny talking to her friends animatedly. She looked excited, and they were all leaning in and smiling. She glanced over at him and he quickly looked down at his tray, stabbing a piece of chicken with his spork.

■ ■ ■

When the final bell rang, Mitch hurriedly stuffed his homework in his backpack and made for the door. He had to practice sax and get his homework done before Dad got home. Then they were going to shop for running shoes and some clothes to practice in and grab dinner. From time to time, their family split up and Mom and Addie had a girls' night and he and Dad had a guys' night. He loved it. Alone time with Dad was rare. He worked a lot and typically they did stuff as a family. It made nights like this even more special.

Mitch jogged across the fields toward his house. He wished he could have gone to practice today. Part of him was nervous about being such a late addition to the team. He hoped his teammates wouldn't resent him for starting a few weeks late. He also hoped he was good enough to make them glad he was part of the team. He'd find out tomorrow.

Assembling the sax before playing it, and disassembling it after, was the only part of playing saxophone that Mitch didn't like. It was a pain. He twisted the brass neck onto the body, and then the mouthpiece onto the cork. He blew a few times before turning the page of his music book to one of the songs Mr. Swan wanted him to improve on. Just as he was about to start playing, his phone, which was holding the pages of his music book in place on the stand, vibrated. He squinted to see the message, hoping he could ignore it and start playing.

Sam Rasmussen - 3:13pm: What are you doing on Saturday?

Mitch knew that Sam knew it was their Homecoming game and dance. The guys talked about it when she was sitting with them last Friday. She was probably hoping that by asking the question, Mitch would ask her to the dance in response. He set the large instrument into its case and picked up the phone, wondering how to say what he knew he needed to say.

Mitch Henry - 3:15pm: Hey Sam! I joined the track team and I'm not sure if I have practice, but if I don't I might ask one of the girls you met on Friday to go to Homecoming with me.

Was it unkind? He didn't actually have plans to ask anyone, it's just the first thing that came to mind. It's not like he knew how he felt about Ginny right now anyway. But he suspected Sam wouldn't give up unless she knew there wasn't a chance. Just like he wouldn't if roles were reversed. He sighed and pressed send.

When a response didn't come, he set the phone back on the music stand and picked up the sax, arranging it and himself to start playing. He slowly played through the song with no mistakes on notes. Now he just needed to get the timing. As he started to play it again, Sam responded.

Sam Rasmussen - 3:19pm: Those girls seemed really nice, I hope you have fun! See you next time our sisters get together.

For a second, Mitch questioned his own sanity. Was it a mistake to let Sam go like this? His eyes fell on the colorful Post-it notes that marked the songs he had to master. What was it his mom sometimes said when she had to turn things down? She had too much on her plate? That's how Mitch felt now. He wasn't sure he could keep up with everything even if he did give up his podcast. Maybe he had to cut down on his lawn and snow business, or narrow his service area.

He played all of the songs, three times each, and then took the stairs two at a time up to his bedroom to work on homework. He was closing his math book when he heard his dad yelling from downstairs. Time to go.

That's when Mitch realized he was supposed to air a podcast tonight. They wouldn't be back early enough for him to prepare a good one. They might not even be home by the time it was supposed to start. He opened his laptop and found the episode that had first been hacked. Many of his new listeners probably hadn't heard that first one. He put his headphones on and pressed the record button.

"Hey everyone, here's a repeat of an oldie but goody. I'll be back live on Thursday. Hope you enjoy it!"

He added the introduction to the beginning of the episode and cued it up to play at 7 p.m. This way something would still play tonight and he didn't have to figure out how to tell everyone he was putting the podcast on hold, maybe indefinitely.

■ ■ ■

Carrying bags from the Nike store, Mitch and Dad walked to the car. The air was cool and the sky was getting dark.

"PastaGina for dinner?" Dad asked, opening the trunk of his car.

They placed the bags on top and around Dad's golf clubs. "Yes!" Mitch said. He loved PastaGina. They had good pasta, but Mitch was obsessed with their hot bread. It just kept coming! As soon as a waiter saw the basket even a little low, a fresh basket would arrive, steaming and smelling of sweet white bread rolls.

They were seated in a large booth. The dining room was dimly lit, candles burned under glass globes on each table. Mitch guessed it was supposed to be romantic or something. Dad was looking at the menu, but Mitch got the same thing every time he came. He was looking around the room at the other diners. That's when he saw Ginny.

She was at a table with her mom and grandma. Mitch had never seen Ginny's grandma before, but recognized her from the many times Rosco had talked about her. Ginny wasn't talking, she was sipping a red drink from a straw while her grandma spoke. It didn't look like any of them were having fun.

A waiter arrived and took their order. When he'd taken their menus and gone, Dad pulled a folded piece of paper out of his back pocket. "The track schedule. Let's see what we're dealing with." He unfolded it and placed it in the middle of the table, sideways, so it wasn't upside down for either of them.

The first track meet was Saturday. The day of the Homecoming dance. Mitch used his pointer finger to go down the line to the times. It started at 9 a.m. He'd be able to go to both the meet and the dance.

"Oh look, this one is in Iowa, that's cool." His dad was pointing to an event a few lines down.

Mitch heard a sort of hiss and looked up. Ginny, her mom, and her grandma were leaving. They'd have to walk right past their booth. He'd decided he would smile and say hi if Ginny looked up. As they got closer he could hear her grandma saying, "I will never understand what you saw in that man. Honestly, Lisbeth, what *were* you thinking?" Mitch focused his gaze on the list of practices and meets, embarrassed at what he'd overheard. Without moving his head, he snuck a look and saw that both Ginny's mom and Ginny looked miserable.

Once they'd passed, Mitch thought about all of the times Ginny had told him how lonely she was without her dad at home. Or that her grandma was mean and seemingly uncaring. He felt ashamed. Ginny, or Rosco, may have not been completely truthful, but he knew her life wasn't easy. She was there for him when he was feeling hopeless about not being able to play sports anymore. She had been his only friend.

An idea started to sprout. He looked at the schedule again, paying close attention to the notes at the bottom of the page, and smiled. When his spaghetti with meatballs and chocolate milk arrived, he knew what he had to do.

23

GINNY

Ginny waited for Mom in the car. She could see her leaning down to Grandma's car window. She was tapping her pointer finger on the top of the car door, as if trying to emphasize a point. Neither woman looked happy. Ginny looked down. Dinner had been a disaster, but there was something different between her and Mom. Something good. She couldn't tell if something had changed with Mom, or with herself, or both.

■ ■ ■

When Ginny had gotten home after school that day, Grandma was still in her kitchen. She was in a particularly sour mood. "Your mother is going to meet us for dinner. She'll come straight from the airport."

Ginny didn't want to talk about Dad's news with Grandma, so she worked on her homework up in her room, and then took Lucky for a walk around the neighborhood. It was the perfect weather for walking. Not too cold, but not hot either.

She'd timed it perfectly. After their walk it was time to go meet Mom. Ginny was so excited to talk to Mom. Dad's note said he and Mom had been discussing the move. Mom would probably have more information and Ginny couldn't wait to find out more.

The car ride to PastaGina had been silent. Grandma was listening to the news and not talking. Ginny looked out the window at the passing houses, and then businesses. She saw Mom the moment they pulled in to the parking lot. She was sitting on a bench outside the door with a wrapped package. Ginny hadn't been this excited to see Mom in a long time. Once they had parked, she ran to Mom and hugged her tight.

Grandma walked swiftly past, into the doors of the restaurant, like she didn't even know them. Mom squeezed Ginny and whispered "Come on" and they followed Grandma in.

Throughout dinner, Ginny and Mom talked excitedly about the program Dad would be leading. Aside from heavy sighs and eye rolls, Grandma barely participated. Before the food came, Mom handed Ginny a package that was clumsily wrapped in brown paper. It clearly wasn't Mom's normally near perfect work.

"I know," Mom said, laughing. "Etienne insisted he wrap it. This one was his idea."

Ginny realized that hearing Etienne's name didn't bother her nearly as much as it did when Dad was completely out of the picture.

She pulled the paper apart and found a football, or soccer, jersey from Etienne's old team. She held it up and looked at the bright colors. It was just her size and she knew it would look great with leggings or jeans.

"Turn it around," Mom said, quietly. She was smiling.

On the back of the jersey, in large blue letters, it said ROSS. Ginny knew she was blushing, or soon would be. Etienne had obviously put a lot of thought into this gift. For the first time, she thought she might actually like to meet this guy.

Grandma let out a laugh. "Well, *that's* rich!"

Ginny folded the jersey and set it in her lap. She hoped Grandma would leave it at that, but feared she wouldn't.

"You have the jersey of your new boyfriend's team with the name of your ex-husband on the back. Ridiculous."

Ginny looked down but could feel her mom bristle.

"Mom, it's Ginny's and my last name too. But no time to argue. Ginny, don't you have homework?"

Mom was looking at Ginny pointedly. "Ahh . . ." Ginny didn't have homework left but she definitely shared Mom's desire to end this dinner. "Yes, I have reading to do."

Grandma scowled at them both. "You said you were *done* with your homework. That is the only reason I let you walk that dog of yours."

Mom stood, and Ginny followed her lead. They waited for Grandma to rise. She did so, slowly, muttering about how unappreciative young people were. She continued to say nasty things until they got outside, when Ginny's mom interrupted Grandma to say, "Ginny, get in the car please. I'll be right there."

Mom was quiet on the ride home. Not in a bad way; Ginny could tell she was just sorting some things out. When they walked into the house, Mom said, "Get your jammies on and then come on back down. I want to talk to you."

Ginny ran upstairs and put on flannel pajama bottoms and a T-shirt. When she got back downstairs, Mom was putting a spoonful of whipped cream on top of two mugs of hot chocolate. She handed one to Ginny and they sat on the couch.

Mom looked nervous and kept her eyes on her own mug. This worried Ginny. Usually, Mom seemed in control. "Honey, sometimes when adults don't know what to do, or they're sad, they kind of shut down and run on auto-pilot. Do you know what I mean?"

Mom looked up and Ginny nodded.

"Ever since Dad and I decided we should separate, and then divorce, I have been running on auto-pilot. Dad and I are a lot like my parents. Remember how fun and loving Grandpa Weber was?"

Ginny did remember. He was one of her favorite people before he died a few years ago. He would get down on the floor to play with her when she was little, he was kind to everyone, and he drew people in. Mom was right. Dad was a lot like Grandpa.

"Dad is so much like my dad, it sometimes broke my heart to see him with you after my dad died. And I am more like Grandma," she started, but Ginny interrupted.

"No, Mom. You are not!" Mom may not have been warm and fuzzy, and she might not have been a talker or known everyone like Dad, but she wasn't mean or cold like Grandma.

Mom smiled but looked sad. "Well, I am in some ways, and I think you've seen that a lot more since Dad moved out. Right?"

Now it was time for Ginny to look down at her mug. Of course she was right. Mom was in and out and tried to be cheery, but something was missing. "I guess," Ginny conceded.

"Since Dad and I separated, I've felt very ashamed. I know we let you down, and I felt like it was my fault. And Grandma didn't help matters. Grandma is in a lot of pain right now, and she's scared about the future. She could have back surgery but she's really nervous about that. The only way she knows how to deal with her pain and her fear is by lashing out at the people she loves most. And we're lucky to be those people right now." At this Mom laughed.

Ginny did too, happy to have something light in this heavy conversation. They both drank from their mugs, achieving matching whipped-cream mustaches. This made them laugh more.

"Listen, Dad and I have talked a lot over the past few weeks. We knew all along that you needed both of us here in Minnesota. Dad has been working on getting this program started for a long time, but we didn't want to get your hopes up. The reason he had to go to Chicago yesterday was that I had a layover there, and we wanted to have dinner and talk about things."

This surprised Ginny. He left her to go meet Mom? She'd always felt like they were three separate ships, passing each other in the night, but never really coming together. Especially not her parents.

"You have taken the brunt of our sadness and shame, and it's not fair. We're both committed to doing better. We're even—" she paused and sipped her cocoa. "We're actually going to therapy to figure out how to do better with you, and together, to co-parent."

Ginny's heart swelled. For the first time in a very long time she felt like she was a kid, and her parents were actually parenting. Her shoulders relaxed and she leaned back into the couch cushions. Her eyes fell on the cable box and she realized it was 7:30 p.m. Halfway through Mitch's show. For a second, she tensed but she was so relieved to be talking, *really* talking to Mom. She took another sip and let thoughts of Mitch and secrets go.

■ ■ ■

Ginny was exhausted. The days with Dad, the news of his moving home, the crazy dinner with Grandma, and the late-night talk she had with Mom had been an emotional roller-coaster. There was more to come, too. Dad was flying in and they were going to have a family dinner tonight. The thought of this was both wonderful and a little nerve-wracking. The three of them hadn't really been together in a long time.

She threw on leggings—there were clean ones in a basket outside her door this morning—and her new jersey. She had practice this morning but Alicia was taking her place at tonight's game. It wasn't like Ginny was sick, or had a crisis; she just wanted to be with her family and find out the details of how this would all work now that Dad was moving home.

"Let's go, Gin," Mom called from downstairs. Ginny put her hair up and grabbed her backpack.

Mom dropped her at the door at the same time Alicia was getting out of her dad's car behind them.

"Did you just get up?" Alicia asked as they walked into school.

Ginny smiled. "Maybe."

Alicia laughed. "Cool jersey, though."

Ginny turned around so she could see ROSS on the back.

"Awesome," Alicia said. "Did you find out anything else about your dad coming back?"

They turned into the gym and dropped their bags on the bleachers that lined the wall. "He's coming for dinner tonight. We're going to talk about," Ginny used her fingers to make air quotes, "the plan."

Alicia put her arm around Ginny's shoulders. "I'm so happy for you!" she said in a squeal.

They got in line and started stretching.

■ ■ ■

As soon as Ginny got home from school she went to her room and opened her laptop. She and Mitch hadn't spoken since Tuesday morning, and that was a short exchange. She needed to tell him what was going on.

Rosco: Hey you...

Lucky, who must have been asleep when she walked in, started barking downstairs. Ginny walked to her bedroom door. "It's just me, Luck," she yelled. She heard him trotting upstairs and soon he was pressing his nose into her thigh, begging for attention. She sat down at her desk again and stared at the screen, petting Lucky's back at the same time.

Nothing. No response. She felt like she was missing something. She never talked to him after Sunday's show. Only that one quick conversation, if you could even call it that, on Monday. And then nothing. She thought about what he'd said. He was joining track. She realized he would be at track practice now. She shut her laptop in frustration and went down to the kitchen.

There was a note on the island from Mom. She'd gone to pick Dad up from the airport. Ginny went to the cupboards in search of a snack. She looked at the options, choosing chocolate rice cakes and peanut butter. As she spread the peanut butter on the rice cakes, she had a thought. What if Mitch *did* like Sam Rasmussen? Maybe *she* was the one he was talking to these days instead of Ginny. She still didn't know how to tell him the truth. Now that felt even harder than it did before. She felt consumed by the changes at home and with her dad moving back. And she still didn't know if she would have to switch schools. It was all so overwhelming.

She settled in front of the TV and turned it on. Maybe she couldn't have both a happy family and Mitch. She chewed thoughtfully, mulling this over. He'd been her support system when she felt like her family was falling apart. Now, things were getting better and she didn't have him to tell. Why couldn't she have both?

24

MITCH

Practice was exhilarating, really hard, and one of the best times Mitch had ever had in his life. He stumbled home on wobbly legs, body drenched in sweat and his face red as a tomato from all of the exertion. He hadn't worked that hard, physically, in years.

He wasn't going to be the star runner. At least not this year, and probably not next year either. He was likely the slowest person on the team, and had the most to learn about the different events. Coach Shields said they wouldn't know which one was best for him for a few days, but that he had some ideas.

He also wouldn't be running on Saturday. He was expected to be there—the whole team had to be there—but he would be watching and helping Coach keep track of times and scores.

But none of it mattered. The people on the team had been welcoming. They all knew his story, especially now that his podcast was so popular. They were grateful to have another runner. He worked his butt off too, which probably helped. Even though he was brand new to track, he ran as hard as he could and did every single thing Coach asked.

Despite Mitch's inexperience, and his slow speed, he knew. He *knew* he had found his sport. Even though there were times he thought he might drop from a heart attack—and even though his legs could barely carry him home—he had loved every second of it. He wasn't even sure he'd be good enough to run in *any* of the meets this year, but he was okay with that. It could be a training year, and he'd have all next summer to practice.

He thought again about what activity to drop in order to do track, and it occurred to him that he'd be willing to drop almost any of them. Well, maybe not sax; he was getting good at that and was in a special ensemble. But the podcast and even mowing lawns? They seemed so much less important.

After showering, and before heading to the basement to practice sax, he checked his computer. Rosco/Ginny had sent him a message after school. He would be talking to her soon enough and he knew dinner would be ready soon. Without responding, he turned for the stairs, smiling.

■ ■ ■

Mitch looked at himself on his computer screen. He always hated how he looked on screens. He heard a ding as Robin logged on. He waved, his actions delayed on the screen, making him wave longer than he needed.

"Hey, Mitch," Robin's tinny voice came through his laptop speakers.

Another ding divided the screen into three. Robin and Josh took up the majority, and Mitch could still see himself in a little box on the lower right hand side.

This was it. Mitch inhaled nervously and started talking.

■ ■ ■

A day had never gone by so slow. Mitch was sure of it. He knew he'd ran faster at today's practice because of the nervous energy that was coursing through his body.

He'd seen his friends throughout the day, but instead of real conversations, they'd exchanged knowing glances and talked about easy things. The weather, assignments they didn't actually care about, what was for lunch, and more. They were all trying not to say anything that could give away the plan.

Thankfully Mitch barely saw Ginny at all. He glimpsed the back of her cheerleading uniform as she ducked into first hour, but that was it. He guessed she might be a little hurt at his neglect lately. That was okay: it actually made avoiding her a lot easier.

Practice was hard. Again, he worked himself as hard as he could, and he could tell it was winning him points with his teammates and Coach. When it was time, Coach released the team, but asked Mitch to come back to his office with him.

Mitch's heart sank. Had he been so distracted that he messed something up in practice? He'd been on the track team for two days and now he was going to get cut? He forgot all about Ginny—and the night ahead of him—and followed Coach Shields inside, his shoulders slumped.

"Have a seat," Coach said.

Mitch dropped into an old brown chair with silver metal arm rests that was unusually uncomfortable. He wondered if the chair was uncomfortable intentionally, to distract from the bad news. It made him even more anxious.

Coach was looking at a piece of paper and nodding. He set it down and removed the glasses he'd put on before reading it. He leaned back in his chair and looked at Mitch. "I see a lot of potential in you," he started.

Any hope Mitch had was dashed. He was obviously being let down easy. His throat tightened and he worried he might actually start crying here in Coach's office.

"I've seen you running over the past year and always thought you should be on a track team, but . . ." Coach let his chair go back to its normal position and he leaned his elbows on his desk.

Mitch braced himself.

"I didn't expect you to work so hard and have such an advanced understanding of the events. I know this might worry you, but I want you suiting up for Saturday's meet. I'd like you to try the 800 meter." He got up from his desk and walked out of his office.

Shocked, Mitch sat completely still in the horrible chair, his fists gripping the metal arm rests. Where had Coach gone? What just happened?

It was a few minutes before Coach strode back into his office, arms full. "Sorry, I thought you followed me out." He dropped the pile he'd been carrying on the desk and start pulling pieces out and handing them to Mitch.

"Kenwood Track Team T-shirt and sweats, Kenwood warm-ups and jacket— you'll wear these over your uniform to all meets—and, finally, your uniform. Your mom listed your size on your registration form, but if any of it doesn't fit, bring it back tomorrow and we'll get you the right size."

Now Mitch's arms were full. He looked down at the unfolded mass of blue and grey clothes and he tried to remember another moment in which he was this proud.

■ ■ ■

This would be the last podcast. At least for a while. Part of him felt bad, like he was leaving his classmates to grapple with their problems alone. But he didn't feel qualified to help everyone and he wasn't sure this was the right way to do it anyway.

Mitch wrote what he planned to say in math class. It was the only class he was far enough ahead in—*thank you, Mom*—that he could zone out but understand exactly what Mrs. Applegren was talking about when he paid attention again.

Robin would be getting to Ginny's anytime. She was going to make sure Ginny listened. Jin, Josh, and Alicia were the only other ones whose parents would let them out that late on a school night. They would meet Mitch at Ginny's at 8 p.m.

He recorded the first half of the podcast after he got home with his pile of team gear. It was part goodbye and thank you for listening, part story about Rosco/Ginny.

He scheduled everything, checked it twice, and shut his laptop.

"There he goes," Dad said from the living room where both he and Mom were working. "Off to woo someone special."

This embarrassed Mitch. He'd had to tell his parents what he was doing, or they'd think it was weird that he was leaving the house when it was getting dark out.

Addie appeared, seemingly out of nowhere. "What? What does that mean? Sam?"

Mitch rolled his eyes. "No, Sherlock. Not Sam."

She followed him around the kitchen as he grabbed a water and then his keys.

"What are you doing?" she pestered.

Mitch stopped, causing Addie to run into the back of him. He turned around, smiled, and said, "None of your business." With that he left through the door that went into the garage.

Sitting on his bike, he pulled his backpack to his front to make sure he had everything he needed. He returned it to his back and rode down the driveway in the dimming light. At the bottom, he took a right, and he was headed to Rosco. Finally.

25

GINNY

Ginny and Robin sat in the kitchen talking to Mom. Robin was asking about France and Mom was telling her about the shopping in Paris. Robin's eyes were wide as Mom described the carts that stood alongside the Seine river that displayed art, scarves, and more.

Ginny noticed the time and pushed her stool away from the island. "Come on, Robin. Time for *Sports with Mitch*."

Robin smiled at Mom and followed Ginny upstairs.

They sat on the floor, Lucky between them, and the song started playing.

Robin leaned back against Ginny's closet door. "So, you haven't talked to Mitch since Tuesday?"

Ginny shook her head. "Maybe he really likes that Sam girl." She thought she saw Robin smile for a second.

"Well, that would be unfortunate," Robin said. "Turn it up!"

Ginny turned the volume on the speaker she had hooked up to her computer's Bluetooth.

"Welcome to the Thursday edition of *Sports with Mitch*. We have a big show for you tonight. Obviously, we will talk sports. We also have a pretty amazing secret being revealed tonight, *and* I have an announcement."

Ginny looked at Robin with confusion.

"You don't know what he's talking about?" Robin asked.

Ginny shook her head and whispered, "No."

The first twenty minutes were all sports. Ginny and Robin tuned it out, instead taking pictures of themselves with Lucky. They were debating how they could make Lucky look more human. They'd tried sunglasses, Ginny's prescription glasses (Mom had not been happy when she walked in on that), and putting Ginny's cheerleading skirt on him. They were on the floor, laughing, when they heard Mitch say, "Okay, now for my announcement." They sat up, alert, and listened.

There was a pause, just silence, and finally Mitch said, "This will be the last episode of *Sports with Mitch*."

Ginny gasped and put her hands to her mouth. Maybe the extra listeners didn't help after all? Maybe he was in trouble for the secrets? She looked to Robin, who looked, well, strange. Ginny looked back to her computer as if Mitch was there talking to her in person.

"I know, what will you do without me? The truth is, I'm going back to playing sports and I just won't have the time for this anymore. Also, for those of you who are long-time listeners, you know it's always been about the sports for me. It's always interesting to hear other people's secrets, it sometimes makes us feel better about our own problems, or we try to help, but that's not why I started this podcast."

Ginny could not believe what she was hearing. He didn't even talk to her about this? Did he tell Sam? Did *she* know about his plan?

"I do," Mitch continued, "have one final secret to share with all of you before I sign off, though. I have to tell you a story first.

"I met a girl online about a year ago. We were both in this programming group and we became friends. She actually turned into one of my best friends. We never met in person, but I talked to her every day."

Ginny scrambled to the computer and turned the volume up. She was transfixed.

"I recently found out that she actually goes to my school. Can you imagine having this amazing online friendship with someone and then finding out they've been sitting at the same lunch table?"

Ginny looked back and realized Robin wasn't there. She must have gone to the bathroom.

"At first I was mad because I thought, 'There is no way she doesn't know who I am. Why didn't she tell me who *she* was?' It took me a couple of days of not talking to her as much to realize that it's kind of the best news ever. One of my very best friends lives here in Kenwood."

What was he saying? Ginny was kneeling on the floor in front of her desk, her hands pressing into her forehead. How did he find out?

"I'm going to see her now. That's it for this edition of *Sports with Mitch*. Rosco, I'll see you soon."

"What?" Ginny croaked. She stood, unsure what to do. She looked in the mirror and saw her confused and worried face looking back at her. Then, the doorbell rang.

The house was quiet. Ginny stood at the top of the stairs, again wondering what had happened to Robin. "Mom?" She called. No answer.

She slowly descended the stairs. The textured glass of their front door made it impossible to see who was standing on the other side. When she reached the door, she looked back toward the kitchen, where her mom had been last time she saw her. She didn't see her there now.

Putting her hand on the knob, she took a deep breath, and turned and pulled. There stood Robin, grinning, and holding a white poster board that said in big letters "MITCH WANTED TO TELL YOU . . ."

Ginny pushed open the storm door and walked outside. Robin moved next to her and Ginny saw Jin standing about ten feet behind Robin with another sign.

"THAT HE KNOWS YOU'RE ROSCO . . ."

Her mind swirled. What was going on? Why was Robin so smiley?

Behind Jin stood Alicia holding another sign. She was smiling too.

"WHICH WORKS OUT BECAUSE . . ."

She moved over and Ginny saw Josh standing farther down the driveway.

"HE HAS A QUESTION FOR ROSCO . . ."

Josh moved over, and in the dark Ginny could see one more white sign down by her mailbox. As she got closer, with Robin, Alicia, Jin, and Josh gathered and walking behind her, she saw Mitch holding the last sign.

"WILL SHE GO TO HOMECOMING WITH ME (AND THESE GUYS TOO)?"

Ginny's mom had once told her a story about Dad throwing her a surprise party when they were still just dating. When they arrived, because Mom wasn't expecting it, she didn't even recognize everyone at first because it was so surprising. It took a little while for it to register that all of her friends were there for *her* and not because of some crazy coincidence. The confusion had been so great that she couldn't comprehend it.

That was how Ginny felt. She stood in front of Mitch, who was starting to shift his weight from side to side. She felt Robin move close to her and take hold of her elbow.

"Gin? You okay?"

Ginny looked around at her friends. They were still smiling but exchanging glances. She looked back at Mitch, who suddenly felt like a stranger. Not a person she'd talked to about almost every single thing in her life.

Embarrassed, she timidly said, "I don't get it."

Nobody said anything, and Mitch let the sign drop to his side, looking defeated.

Ginny's mind, which had been at once swirling and the next moment felt full of mud, started to clear. "I mean, how did you know it was me?"

Mitch tilted his head toward her mailbox. "I left my bill on Monday and other mail fell out. There was an envelope . . ."

" . . . addressed to Rosco. Right," Ginny interrupted, remembering her nickname written in big black letters in Dad's handwriting.

"So?" Josh asked. "Are you going to come to the dance with us?"

The others joined in. "Yeah, you can't leave us hanging," said Jin, mock punching Ginny in the arm.

As it sunk in, Ginny began to smile. Was this actually happening? She looked back at Mitch, who looked hopeful. He gave her a half smile.

"Yes. I'll go to Homecoming with you," she said, starting to feel giddy. "We can celebrate your sports comeback!"

The guys high-fived, and Alicia, Robin, and Ginny shared a group hug.

Ginny stared at herself in the mirror that hung on the back of her closet door. The navy dress and heels made her look and feel like a princess. She was waiting for Mom to find a necklace for her to wear when there was a soft knock at the door.

"Come in," Ginny said, still staring at her reflection. Grandma walked in wearing a pink argyle golf ensemble and holding a deep-blue velvet box.

"Grandma," Ginny said, stepping back from the mirror. "I didn't know you were here."

Grandma sat stiffly in the chair at Ginny's desk and let out a breath. "When I heard you were getting ready for your first dance, I decided I could skip golf this afternoon." She pointed at the bed and Ginny obligingly sat down.

"Your grandfather used to travel a lot for work. We were lucky, I got to go with him on many trips, but sometimes my work schedule wouldn't allow me to accompany him. Once, he had to go to Paris, but I had an important project I was working on and couldn't go. I was so upset. Like your mother, I *love* Paris." She adjusted how she was sitting and grimaced. Ginny involuntarily winced.

"He was gone for only four days, but it felt like forever because he was in this city I love without me. When he got back, he gave me these." Grandma handed Ginny the velvet box. "I think he felt bad about having to leave me at home!"

Ginny lifted the lid and inside was a delicate silver chain with a sparkling round blue gem and a pair of earrings with the same blue stones. She looked up and saw Grandma smiling. Ginny hadn't seen her smile like that in a very long time.

"Oh goodness," Grandma said, slowly and carefully standing. "Your grandpa would be tickled pink to see you wearing these. Come on, we don't have all day, let's put them on."

Ginny stood and Grandma took the necklace and fastened it around her neck. She handed her the earrings and Ginny put them in. They looked in the mirror together. Grandma put her hands on Ginny's bare shoulders and whispered, "You look lovely. Now. Off you go." She swatted Ginny's bottom and left her standing alone. Ginny took one last look at her reflection, nearly transfixed by what she saw, and then followed Grandma out.

■ ■ ■

Ginny, Robin, Alicia, and Emily took selfies in Ginny's driveway. Ginny twirled in her navy dress, Robin posed in her emerald-green dress, Alicia—who finally asked Jin to the dance and received "woman what took you so long?" for an answer—flashed the peace sign in her purple satin dress and heels, and Emily, who was going to the dance without a date, danced around in a black tutu skirt, a black-and-white striped shirt, and ballet flats. Mitch, Josh, and Jin were meeting them at the school entrance.

After taking pictures until there were no poses left untried, Mom drove them to school. The guys were taking pictures on the benches in front of the entrance.

"*What,*" Emily said as they got out of the car, "are they doing?"

Josh, Jin, and Mitch were striking serious poses. "It looks like they're pretending they're mobsters from old movies or something," said Robin, shaking her head. Josh noticed the girls and waved. Mitch and Jin quickly dropped the poses and they met the girls at the door.

Ginny still felt shy around Mitch. It was strange. She felt like he knew her better than almost anyone, but the "in real life" Mitch still made her a bit nervous. "You look nice," she said when he got to her side.

"So do you," he said, and quickly added, "you *all* look really pretty." Ginny's stomach flipped. She couldn't believe she was actually here. With Mitch. With Sportstatsguy.

The gym had been transformed into a fantasy land. The wooden bleachers had been collapsed and pushed into the walls. Streamers, balloons, confetti, and large swaths of metallic material hung from the ceiling and on the walls. Colorful lights zoomed around the room, and a DJ stood behind a large console on the stage. He was playing a song that had just come out, and that Ginny and Robin loved.

"This is our jam," Robin said, grabbing Ginny's arm. "We've gotta go dance."

Josh jerked his head toward the dance floor and Mitch, Jin, Alicia, and Emily followed.

As Ginny and Robin danced, she wondered why people wore high heels to dances. They weren't very comfortable. She looked up and saw that they'd been joined by everyone else. Mitch danced his way over to her. He was wearing dark-grey dress pants, a yellow-and-white-checked button-down shirt, and a yellow-and-grey tie. With Adidas. He wasn't a great dancer. Ginny laughed; he reminded her of her dad trying to dance at family weddings. Never good, but always funny.

"Mitch, my man," Jin yelled over the music. "I think you should probably stick to track. A dancer you are not."

Instead of being deterred, Mitch intensified his dance moves and grinned. His arms and legs flying. By the end of the song, nearly all of them were dripping with sweat. The DJ switched songs, and a slow one came on. A lot of people left the dance floor, but Robin grabbed Josh to dance. Mitch looked at Ginny and she felt butterflies in her stomach.

Ginny had only ever slow danced with Dad. When she was little, he let her stand on his feet while they danced. Mitch wasn't as tall as Dad, and with her heels, Ginny was almost his same height.

Mitch put his hands at Ginny's waist, and she put hers on his shoulders. Mitch cleared his throat and said, "I'm sorry, I really am a terrible dancer."

"It's okay," said Ginny. "You're also terrible at Fortnite but I don't hold it against you."

"She got you there, bro," said Jin, who was dancing with Alicia next to them. Mitch punched his arm and turned Ginny to face a different direction.

They danced in silence for a while. It didn't feel awkward, it felt nice, and Ginny's nerves had calmed. She felt comfortable with him and could tell he felt the same. As the song faded and the base of the next song began to thump, Mitch pulled Ginny into a bear hug. It was as if the rest of the gym fell away and it was only Ginny and Mitch floating above an empty room. He hugged her tight and whispered, "Would you mind if I called you Rosco?" Ginny felt a rush of emotion. Everything she'd hoped would happen actually *did*. Even if there were some bumps along the way. She shook her head and hoarsely said no. Mitch loosened his grip and kissed her on the cheek. And just like that, her friends and classmates reappeared, and she felt like she was back on earth. With Mitch.

26

GINNY

Ginny got out of Mom's car and smoothed her cheerleading skirt. She took a deep breath, surprised at how nervous she was. It's not like she was meeting up with strangers.

A yellow glow came from the large windows of The Drip. She could see Ms. Kelly holding her new baby, and Julie was behind the counter scooping up ice cream. She scanned the tables and found the one she was looking for.

She walked in the door, waving at Ms. Kelly and Julie, and pulled a chair out at the corner table.

Becca looked up from her sundae and pressed her lips.

"Hi, Ginny," Lily offered in her nasal voice.

Becca set her spoon in the bowl and said, "You've got us here. What do you want?"

Ginny wondered why it had seemed so important lately to tell Becca it was *she* who recorded and aired her plans to mess with Josh and Robin. She was getting used to a new normal of having Dad around, going between his new house and Mom's, and being Mitch's . . . well . . . she wasn't quite sure if she was his girlfriend yet, but they were definitely close friends in real life now too in addition to online. As things felt better and more stable in her own life, she'd felt worse and worse about the hacking and the fact that it had actually hurt people.

After another deep breath she said, "It was me."

"*What* was you?" Becca asked.

"I am the one who recorded what you said at that football game. It was an accident. I was recording the squad doing cheers. You guys must have just been standing really close to the camera."

Becca's mouth dropped.

"Wait, it was you? But how did you get it on Mitch's show? He says he didn't know about it." Lily's questions came quick.

"I *knew* that idiot was lying," seethed Becca.

"No!" Ginny worried about this. She didn't want Mitch to be blamed. "No," she said again. "I hacked into his podcast."

Both Becca and Lily looked at Ginny like she must be very stupid to think they'd believe that.

"No, seriously. I'm pretty good at, you know, tech stuff."

Lily looked at her, brow furrowed. "But," she started, then paused. "Why would you tell us this?"

When Ginny and Mitch had the chance to talk alone, about when she realized it was him, and reconciling their online and real lives, she'd admitted to him that she'd been the hacker. He was shocked, and a little upset actually. It took a few conversations, at lunch, or after he'd finished their lawn, for them both to feel okay about it and comfortable with each other. Online and off. But there had been a growing discomfort with the fact that some people still didn't know what she'd done.

The hardest person to admit it to was Robin. She actually stopped talking to Ginny for two full days. It was a weekend, but Ginny spent that time worrying that she'd lost her best friend. And for what? On Sunday, she had her mom drop her off at Robin's and she begged for forgiveness.

Becca and Lily were the last people she needed to talk to. After this, everything was out in the open. The bad stuff and the good. Which felt so much better than holding things in.

"I am just really, really sorry. I wasn't thinking and I know it was hard for you guys. People were jerks to you, and it was my fault." Becca's usual surly facial expression turned to sadness. Ginny's heart sunk.

"If there is ever anything I can do to make it up to you, I . . ."

Becca cut her off. "I don't need anything from you. You suck." She pushed her chair back and walked out the door.

Ginny expected Lily to follow, but she stayed seated.

"Sorry about Becca," Lily said quietly. "Her parents are getting divorced and things at her house have been really bad for a couple of years. That's why she acts like this."

Ginny was surprised to hear Lily talk this way. She'd always had the impression that Becca was just a mean person who bossed Lily around. Turns out, Becca was struggling at home like Ginny had been. Lily was just trying to help. Just as Ginny was trying to help Mitch when she exposed Becca, and Robin. Ginny sighed.

Lily got up and gathered Becca's and her own bowls. "Thanks for saying you're sorry. I forgive you. And I think Becca will too. Nobody ever apologizes to her. You might be the first." She walked to a garbage can and threw away the paper bowls, then she waved at Ginny as she followed Becca out the door.

■ ■ ■

Ginny got under her covers and opened her laptop. She was playing with some new programming software and was having trouble figuring something out. As she launched the system, Ginny opened Chatter. She had a message waiting for her in her mailbox.

She opened it, and there were the two words that had become her favorites.

"Hey you..."

ACKNOWLEDGMENTS

I owe a great deal of thanks to many people. First, to my husband Matt, who supported my going back to school for an MFA, provided tough love to keep me working (when nothing seemed to be working), and has encouraged me since the beginning of this process. To my girls who have given me ideas, both by simply being themselves and when I've asked for them, and have understood when I needed to close my office door to write. To my parents and brother who have been supportive of every single thing I've ever tried to accomplish. And my girlfriends who are the best girlfriends one could ever hope for – Alia, Annie, April, Ginger, Heidi, Holly, Jody, Kris, Patti, and Sara.

Thank you to Donna Freitas and Eliot Schrefer for showing me the way to middle grade. Thank you for your guidance, tough love, and encouragement as I started this book. Thank you to Daphne Benedis-Grab and Brooks Becker for your editing expertise. And thank you to Dan Burdeski for your art!

A special thanks to Fletch for being my reference for all things middle grade boy.

ABOUT THE AUTHOR

Carrie Monroe O'Keefe lives in Minneapolis with her husband, two daughters, and Goldendoodle Sullivan. She graduated from Hamline University and received her MFA in writing for young adults from Fairleigh Dickinson University.

This is her first novel.

Follow Carrie at:
www.carriemonroeokeefe.com
Instagram: @monroeokeefe
Twitter: @cmonroeokeefe
Facebook: https://www.facebook.com/AuthorCarrieMonroe OKeefe/

Made in the USA
Middletown, DE
05 February 2019